Campaign • 39

Little Big Horn 1876

Custer's last stand

Peter Panzeri • Illustrated by Richard Hook

Series editor Lee Johnson • *Consultant editor* David G Chandler

First published in Great Britain in 1995 by
Osprey Publishing, Midland House, West Way, Botley,
Oxford OX2 0PH UK
44-02 23rd St, Suite 219, Long Island City, NY 11101, USA
Email: info@ospreypublishing.com

CIP Data for this publication is available from the British Library

ISBN 978 1 85532 458 9

Military Editor: Lee Johnson
Designed by the Black Spot

Colour bird's - eye view illustrations by Peter Harper.
Cartography by Micromap.
Wargaming Little Big Horn by Peter F. Panzeri Jr.

Fimset in Great Britain.
Printed in China through World Print Ltd.

11 12 13 14 15 25 24 23 22 21 20 19 18 17 16

The Woodland Trust
Osprey Publishing is supporting the Woodland Trust, the UK's leading woodland conservation charity, by funding the dedication of trees.

Osprey Publishing is part of the Osprey Group.

www.ospreypublishing.com

AUTHOR'S NOTE

All place names in this account are referred to by their current descriptions, such as Reno Hill, and Battle Ridge; they had no such names before 1876. Little Big Horn is correctly spelled as either two or three words. It is spelled herein as three separate words except where directly quoted. For the purpose of clarity, the regular Army commissioned rank is used in this account, except when part of a direct quote. Nearly all of the officers in this campaign had held field grade 'Brevet' rank during the American Civil War, and were still addressed with those titles by many in either a social or complementary fashion. (It is sometimes amusing to perceive which early 'historical' accounts are prejudiced by noting whether regular Army or Brevet titles are used.) Many Indians had several names, and there were many of the same name; the most common names known are used, and those particularly frustrating are omitted for convenience.

All sequential times are calculated by the author by reconciling and cross referencing those given in various accounts and time-space experiments on the battlefield.

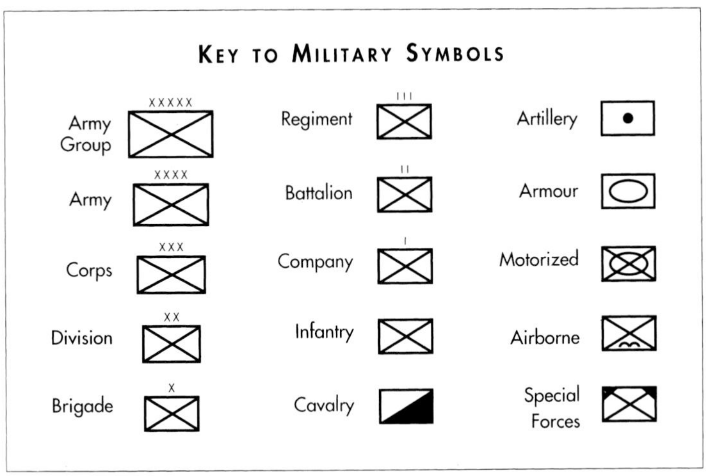

CONTENTS

THE WARPATH TO 1876

By 6.00 p.m. on 25 June 1876, 210 troopers of the US 7th Cavalry Regiment lay dead, scattered about a hillside in southern Montana. Their commander, a US army lieutenant-colonel named George Armstrong Custer, lay with them. Four miles upstream, over 40 other troopers were also dead. They had all perished at the hands of Sioux and Cheyenne warriors in what is now called the 'Battle of The Little Big Horn'. The Native American name for the battle is 'The Greasy Grass'.

The Battle of the Little Big Horn was the apex of the western Indian Wars in North America – the climax of a fascinating military campaign led, on both sides, by some of the most charismatic, colourful and truly controversial personalities in American military history. It was a campaign unsurpassed in the ferocity and savagery of its combat. The Little Big Horn battle was a tactical victory for the American Northern Plains tribes, but it brought on strategic defeat. Above all, it was a classic military disaster, known the world over as 'Custer's Last Stand'.

In the 1860s the Teton Sioux tribes of the great plains roamed and reigned supreme, hunting buffalo in the Dakota and Wyoming territories. The Teton Sioux were early occupants of the Minnesota and Mid-West region, but they were continuously pushed west by the white expansion across North America. The warlike Sioux expelled the Crow tribes (the previous inhabitants) to the west and north. Their ancestral cousins, the Cheyenne, also migrated west, occupying the Southern Great Plains.

In 1863, in the midst of the American Civil War, white expansion once again threatened the Sioux domain. A gold rush in western Montana prompted pioneering of the Bozeman Trail, which cut through the heart of the Sioux buffalo hunting grounds. By 1866 the Army had built three forts (Reno, Kearny, and C.F. Smith) along the Bozeman Trail to protect those migrating west. This encroachment on the Sioux touched off hostilities that were later called Chief Red Cloud's War.

View of Deep Ravine looking west from Custer Hill. A trail of markers run from the hill down toward the ravine, where 30-40 troopers from Custer's command were killed and are supposedly still buried. (J. Thompson)

The only Native American chief ever to go to war and win against the government of the United States of America was the Oglala Sioux Chief Red Cloud. He rose to prominence uniting various bands to halt the white exodus, and was supported by such aspiring leaders as Crazy Horse and Rain in the Face. From 1866 to 1868 the Sioux interrupted movement along the trail and threatened the isolated Army forts.

On 21 December 1866, near Fort Phil Kearny, Captain William J. Fetterman was lured into an ambush. Fetterman, who had once boasted he could ride through the entire Sioux nation with 80 soldiers, met an overwhelming force of warriors led by Red Cloud, and was killed along with exactly 80 men.

By August 1867 the Army had managed to win victories at the Wagon Box and Hayfield battles, but the Bozeman Trail was still hopelessly untenable, and construction of the Union Pacific Railroad made it unnecessary. The US Government decided to abandon the forts, and they negotiated a treaty with Red Cloud at Fort Laramie in 1868. Red Cloud proved to be an effective warrior and a shrewd politician: he signed the treaty only after the forts had been emptied and burned by his exultant warriors.

Oglala Sioux war party mounted on their best ponies, armed to the teeth, and resplendent in their war paint and feather bonnets. These braves embody the spirit of their warrior culture. (Denver Public Library)

UNCEDED TERRITORY

The Little Big Horn Campaign and 1876 Sioux war were in and about that part of the American Great Plains referred to as the 'Unceded Territory'. It included the Powder River basin, stretching from the Rocky and Big Horn Mountains in the west to the Great Sioux Reservation along the Missouri River in the east. By the mid-19th century this region was the principal grazing land for the last of the North American buffalo herds.

The Fort Laramie Treaty set aside the Great Sioux Reservation (all of present day South Dakota west of the Missouri River), with the Sioux drawing rations from several 'Agencies' along the Missouri River. Sioux

Sitting Bull, Hunkpapa Sioux. He was primarily a 'medicine man', the spiritual and political leader of the defiant Sioux. His charismatic leadership and unique spiritual medicine united the various Sioux nations and also a large contingent of Northern Cheyenne. He advocated a return to the 'old ways', and prophesied a defeat of the soldiers. Sitting Bull belonged to the Kit-Fox 'warrior society' and had a reputable war record. By 1876 he was about 45 years old, and left the actual fighting to the younger war chiefs such as Gall, Lame White Man and Crazy Horse. (Little Big Horn Battlefield National Monument)

who rejected any government control or Agency provisions (over 3,000 Sioux and 400 Cheyenne) roamed free in the Unceded Territory. The bands of warriors who remained there were intent on continuing the traditional nomadic lifestyle of the Plains Indians. By 1870 Chief Red Cloud had retired to reservation life, and the 'non-treaty' Indians began to look to new leaders for inspiration. The dominant personality was not a chief, but a 'medicine man' or spiritual leader. His name was Sitting Bull. He insisted

Outa Ammo Outa Luck *by Clyde Heron. As Custer wrote of the Fetterman fight in Life on the Plains "... being short of ammunition and seized with panic at this event and the great numerical strength of the Indians, attempted to retreat, but the mountainees and old soldies, who had learned that a movement from Indians in an engagement was equivalent to death". This fate befell both Reno's and Custer's commands.*

on isolation from whites and strict adherence to cultural and spiritual practices. His reputation and influence grew as he gathered the support of leaders such as Gall, Spotted Eagle and the most uncompromising of all, Crazy Horse.

Many Indians began leaving the Agencies to return to the 'old ways' advocated by Sitting Bull. Some traded and drew rations from the Agencies in winter and hunted with the non-treaty bands in the summer. The area was also a refuge for raiding parties into the Montana and Platte settlements. The warlike Sioux and Cheyenne continuously skirmished, with Crow and Shoshone tribes, with railroad surveying expeditions and their Army escorts, and even with each other. The Unceded Territory, a thorn in the flesh of western expansion, was earmarked for eventual white control. As the railroad branched out further and the buffalo disappeared, so would the problem of the non-Agency Sioux and Cheyenne.

UNCONTROLLED EXPANSION

This supposedly self-resolving problem was viewed with a greater sense of urgency by 1874. A military expedition, led by Lt.Col. George Armstrong Custer and his 7th Cavalry Regiment, was dispatched into the heavily forested Black Hills of South Dakota. The official mission was to find a suitable Army post location for monitoring the Sioux, but it also included mineral surveyors. Rumours of gold were confirmed, and a gold rush rapidly developed, causing great problems for the Indians and for the Army.

The Black Hills were square in the centre of the Great Sioux Reservation. By early 1875 two major mining towns, Deadwood and Custer City, were thriving in the hills, despite Indian agitation. The government could not buy the Black Hills from the Agency Sioux chiefs, who were heavily influenced and threatened by the non-treaty warriors, but it ceased trying to keep civilians out of the area.

It was clear that the followers of Sitting Bull were blocking the sale of the Black Hills. Government officials of the Grant administration and the Department of the Interior decided to force them to the reservations and bring them under Federal control. This mission was assigned to the United States Army.

The persona of George Armstrong Custer became immortal, even mythical, after the Little Big Horn disaster. A highly controversial figure throughout his life, he has become larger than life in the century of speculation since his death. Most of what is written about him is clouded by contradicting descriptions from those who sought to exonerate, blame or eulogise. (Little Big Horn Battlefield National Monument)

PLANS AND PREPARATIONS

'... we were up against it from the start.' CRAZY HORSE

On 9 November 1875 Inspector E.C. Watkins of the US Indian Bureau completed his investigation on the Indian situation in the Black Hills. His report to the Commissioner of Indian Affairs in Washington D.C. blamed a certain rebellious faction of Hunkpapa Sioux, Oglala Sioux and Northern Cheyenne who, detesting Indian Agency corruption and widespread deprivation, had rejected the reservations to live in what they considered their homelands. These 'roamers' were labelled a hostile threat to the western expansion.

An ultimatum was issued on 6 December 1875 for those still in the Unceded Territory. Despite severe weather, Indian agents were sent to notify the non-Agency villages to 'return to their reservations by 31 January 1876, on penalty of being considered hostile'.

These 'hostiles' had sought refuge in the richest of hunting grounds. They had ample buffalo meat and were wealthy in horses and robes. They

US ARMY AND INDIAN ALLIES DIVISION OF THE MISSOURI, JUNE 1876

DIVISION OF THE MISSOURI
(Maj.Gen. Phillip H. Sheridan)
Headquarters, Chicago, Illinois

DEPARTMENT OF DAKOTA
(Brig.Gen. (Brevet Maj.Gen.) Alfred H. Terry)
Headquarters, Saint Paul Minnesota

DEPARTMENT OF DAKOTA
Dakota Column
(Brig.Gen. Alfred H. Terry)
(52 Officers, 879 Men,
3 Gatling Guns, 150 Wagons)
6th Infantry *(Maj. Orlando H. Moore)*
7th Cavalry *(Lt. Col. George A. Custer)*
Steamer FAR WEST *(Capt. Grant Marsh)*
Steamer JOSEPHINE *(Capt. Mart Coulson)*

DEPARTMENT OF DAKOTA
Montana Column
(Col. John Gibbons, 7th Infantry)
Fort Ellis, Montana
(approximately 450 Men)
Capt. Freeman's Battalion, 7th Infantry
2nd Cavalry *(Maj. James S. Brisbin)*

Little Powder, Arapaho war chief. The Arapaho were not normally allied with the Sioux and Cheyenne. Little Powder's band of warriors joined the fight after being 'disarmed and detained'. There were many rival factions within the camp. They were united by Sitting Bull's spiritual 'medicine' and their zeal to fight. (J. H. Foust, Brust Collection)

had continued to trade with white enterprisers, and thus were well-armed with rifles, revolvers and ammunition. They were defiant of the ultimatum.

That same month, the Great Sioux Reservation suffered a grievous famine. Caused by a corrupt system, the famine only strengthened the resolve of many to depart the reservations as soon as weather permitted. On 18 January 1876 an embargo was enforced, restricting the sale of all arms and ammunition on the reservations. This signalled a government intent to commence hostilities.

It is ironic that the Indians, with strategic defeat at stake, had no unified strategy by the very nature of their culture. Their general unifying goals were simply self preservation and occupation of the Unceded Territory. In response to Army initiatives, the winter roamers began banding together for protection.

Sitting Bull motivated his followers through spiritual leadership, while his disciple chiefs advocated and executed warfare on a tactical level. They led by pure charisma, bravery and, above all, by example. Many recalled Red Cloud's victory in 1868, but without the desire or similar ability to negotiate, the 1876 resistance was doomed. Much had changed in ten years. The post-war western expansion was on in earnest. The Unceded Territory was much less remote. The economy was growing. Steamboats navigated the waterways, and railroads reached further.

FEDERAL PLANS

'Unless they can be caught before early spring, they cannot be caught at all.'

GENERAL PHILLIP H. SHERIDAN

In the spring of 1876, General Phillip H. Sheridan, Division of Missouri Commander, ordered three Army columns, totalling 2,500 men, into south-eastern Montana territory. Their mission was to converge on and break up the concentration of hostile Sioux and Cheyenne believed to be in the Big Horn Valley. (U.S. National Archives)

General Phillip H. Sheridan was the Division of Missouri Commander, and his immediate superior was General of the Army William T. Sherman. Both had fought under General Ulysses S. Grant during the American Civil War. In 1876, with Grant as President, the three were collectively dictating policy and intent upon a military solution to the Sioux problem.

On 8 February 1876, after waiting for the ultimatum deadline to expire, Sheridan ordered his subordinate department commanders, Generals Terry and Crook, to 'prepare for operations against the hostiles'. Their mission was to converge on and break up the concentration of hostile Sioux and Cheyenne believed to be in the Big Horn Valley and force them back to the reservations.

In campaigns over the previous ten years these hostile bands had proved to be extremely elusive. During the summer months they were always more mobile than Army forces and were able to scatter if closely pursued. Winter campaigns had become the established method of defeating them. Sheridan's orders were intended to initiate a winter campaign with three columns, two of Terry's and one of Crook's.

Only General Crook, Commander of the Department of the Platte, took to the field before the end of winter. Those forces under Terry, Commander of the Department of Dakota, were themselves delayed by severe weather and also by Terry's logistical worries. The Indian Bureau estimated that between 400 and 800 hostile warriors were dispersed in winter camps

WINTER PRELUDE, MARCH-APRIL 1876

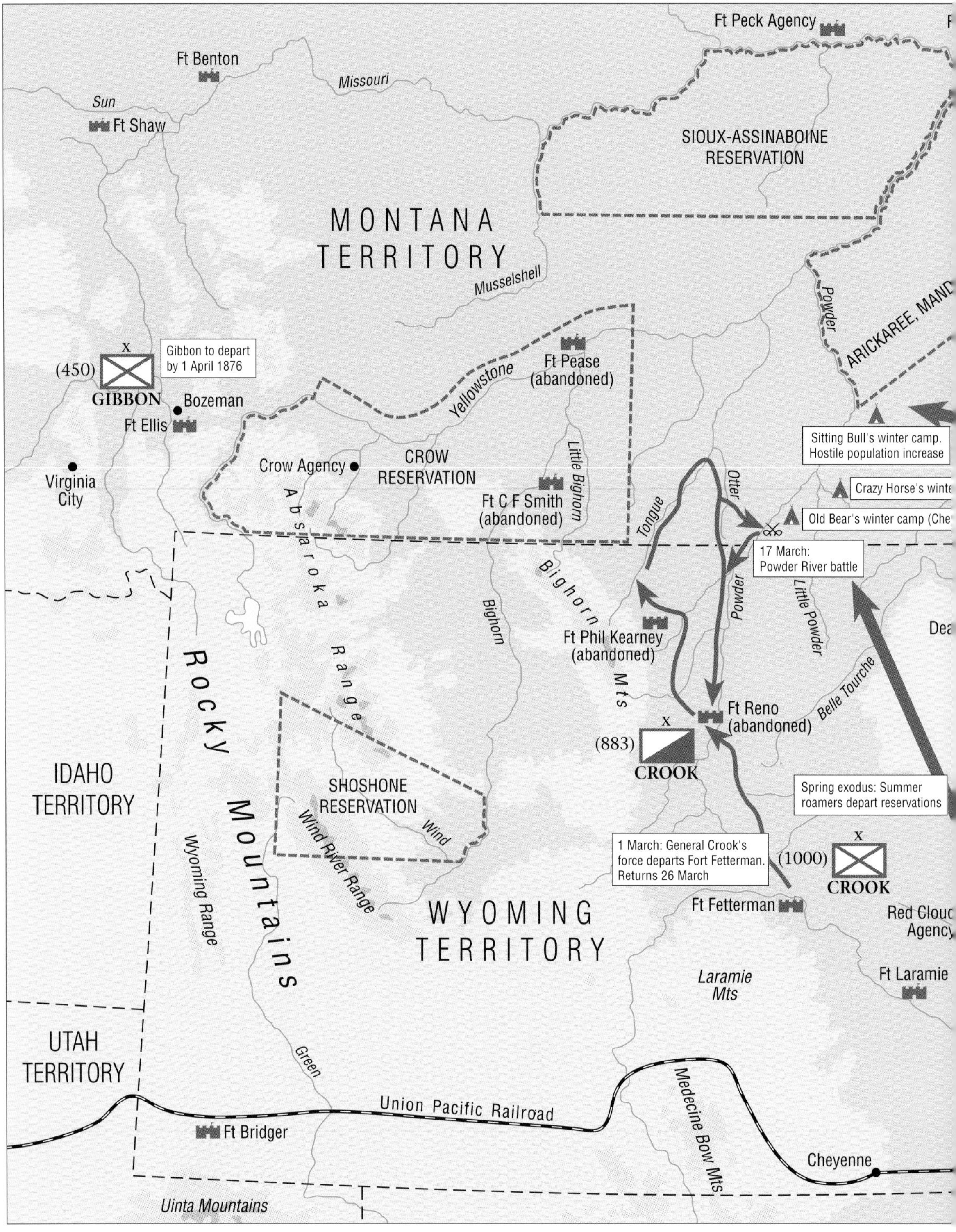
Ft Peck Agency
Ft Benton
Missouri
Sun
Ft Shaw
SIOUX-ASSINABOINE RESERVATION
MONTANA TERRITORY
Musselshell
Powder
ARICKAREE, MAND
Gibbon to depart by 1 April 1876
(450)
GIBBON
Bozeman
Ft Ellis
Yellowstone
Ft Pease (abandoned)
Virginia City
Crow Agency
CROW RESERVATION
Little Bighorn
Ft C F Smith (abandoned)
Absaroka Range
Tongue
Otter
Sitting Bull's winter camp. Hostile population increase
Crazy Horse's winte
Old Bear's winter camp (Che
17 March: Powder River battle
Bighorn
Bighorn Mts
Powder
Little Powder
Ft Phil Kearney (abandoned)
Rocky Mountains
Ft Reno (abandoned)
Belle Fourche
Dea
(883)
CROOK
IDAHO TERRITORY
SHOSHONE RESERVATION
Wind
Wind River Range
Wyoming Range
Spring exodus: Summer roamers depart reservations
1 March: General Crook's force departs Fort Fetterman. Returns 26 March
(1000)
CROOK
Ft Fetterman
Red Clouc Agency
WYOMING TERRITORY
Laramie Mts
Ft Laramie
UTAH TERRITORY
Green
Medecine Bow Mts
Union Pacific Railroad
Ft Bridger
Cheyenne
Uinta Mountains

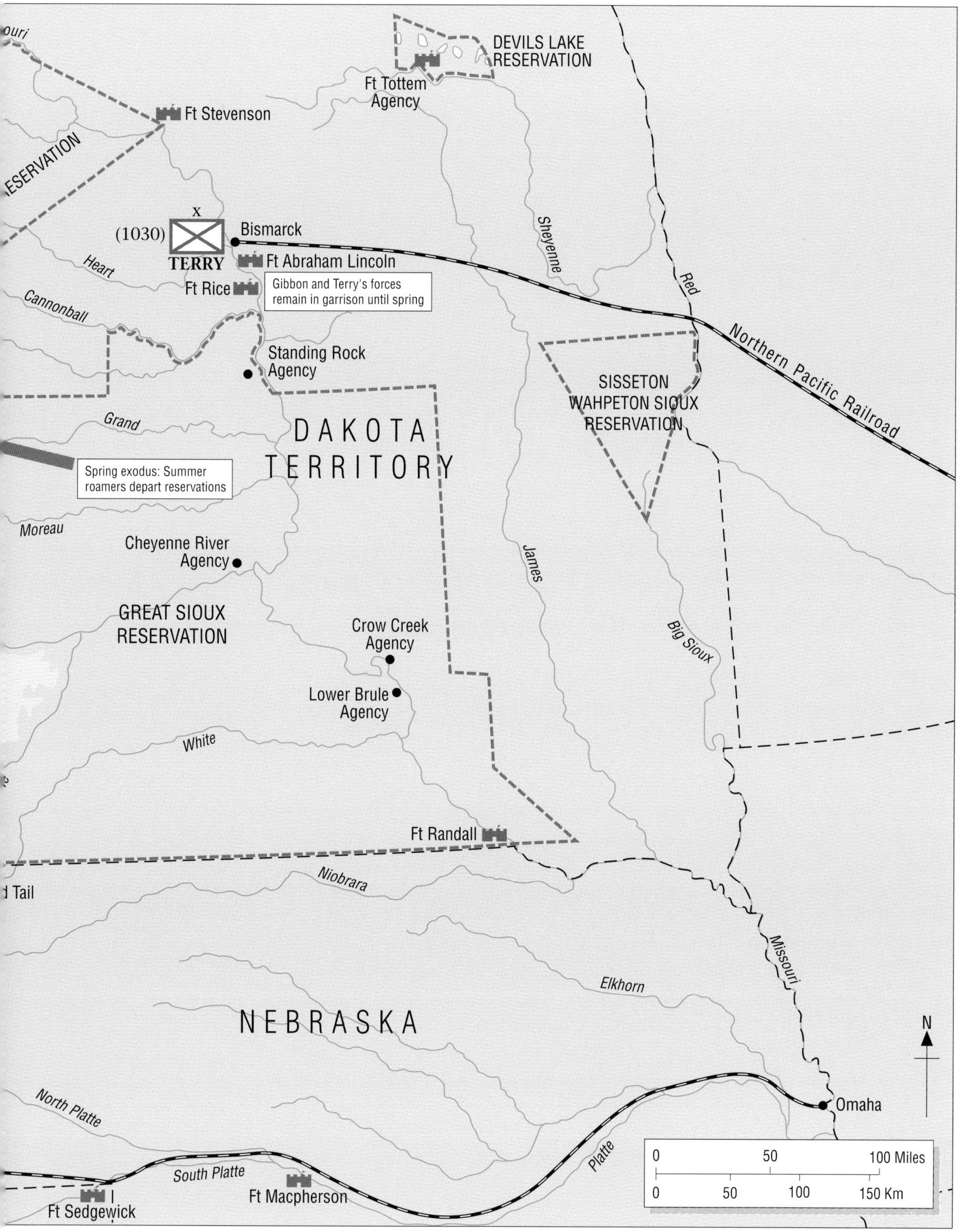
ouri
ESERVATION
Ft Stevenson
DEVILS LAKE RESERVATION
Ft Tottem Agency
x
(1030)
TERRY
Bismarck
Ft Abraham Lincoln
Heart
Ft Rice
Gibbon and Terry's forces remain in garrison until spring
Cannonball
Sheyenne
Red
Northern Pacific Railroad
Standing Rock Agency
SISSETON WAHPETON SIOUX RESERVATION
Grand
DAKOTA TERRITORY
Spring exodus: Summer roamers depart reservations
Moreau
Cheyenne River Agency
James
GREAT SIOUX RESERVATION
Crow Creek Agency
Big Sioux
Lower Brule Agency
White
Ft Randall
Niobrara
d Tail
Missouri
Elkhorn
NEBRASKA
N
North Platte
Omaha
South Platte
Platte
Ft Macpherson
Ft Sedgewick
0 50 100 Miles
0 50 100 150 Km

After Crook's winter raid, small bands of roamers began to consolidate with Sitting Bull and Crazy Horse for protection. These two tepees have artwork commemorating the Sioux victory over Custer at the Battle of the Little Big Horn. (Little Big Horn Battlefield National Monument)

across the Unceded Territory. This estimate is fairly accurate, but accounts only for the winter roamers. The numbers would swell in the spring.

POWDER RIVER RAID

'Bullets and casualties were then bestowed upon us with a will that showed plainly we were not to sweep the field without paying a penalty.'

CORRESPONDENT ROBERT E. STRAHORN, BATTLE OF THE POWDER RIVER, 17 MARCH 1876

Despite blizzards and sub-zero temperatures, Crook's force was heavily scouted by the hostiles, and the cattle herd was stampeded on the second day. After ten days of searching, they came upon an Indian camp along the Powder River Valley. It was Old Bear's camp of about 110 lodges and up to 250 warriors, including Little Wolf, Two Moon and He Dog. Six companies (300 men) were sent to attack the village. The Indians fled to nearby bluffs overlooking the village and began to return fire. In the face of determined hostile resistance the troopers were ordered to burn the camp, destroy all stores and then withdraw. Four soldiers were killed and six wounded during the engagement, and one wounded trooper was abandoned. The warriors followed and managed to recapture most of their herd.

The Sioux and Cheyenne survivors of the Powder River battle were without protection from the extreme cold, and after several days of exposure they combined with Crazy Horse's camp. News of the raid spread amongst all the Indians and served as a clear warning that the Army was intent on waging total war. As the spring grass came, the Indian bands continued to join together for protection.

After their failure at Powder River, it would be two months before Crook could refit his forces for another offensive. His independent Army column had failed in a winter attack against a weakened foe; a summer campaign would be necessary.

THE OPPOSING LEADERS

Brigadier General Alfred H. Terry was concerned he would not catch the hostiles. Finding and engaging the largest concentration possible was the highest priority. Unaware of Gen. Crook's repulse, Terry released Custer and his 7th Cavalry Regiment to move independently. Custer received written orders to approach the Little Big Horn Valley from the south, while Terry approached from the north. (U.S. National Archives)

General Sheridan did not name an overall field commander for the 1876 campaign, nor did he give instructions for tactical co-ordination between the two departments. Generals Crook and Terry were to be considered 'co-equal' department commanders. His decision not to unify tactical and operational command reveals his disregard for Sioux combat potential. It also clearly illustrates the disruptive effect clashes of personality can have on the effective prosecution of a campaign.

The overbearing and energetic Brigadier General George Crook had been a cavalry division commander in the Civil War, and headed the Army of West Virginia during Sheridan's Shenandoah Campaign. He had also graduated from West Point in 1852, one year ahead of Phil Sheridan, and the two were friends. Brigadier General Alfred H. Terry was a 49-year-old veteran of Civil War accomplishment, but this was his first campaign in 11 years, and his first fighting Indians. Subordinate to Terry was Colonel John Gibbon, the 49-year-old commander of the 7th Infantry Regiment and the District of Montana.

Perhaps the most unpredictable element was Custer himself. Since his spectacular death on the Little Big Horn, George Armstrong Custer has become a controversial American folk legend. He is portrayed in every manner, from saint to devil. Custer's own writings are equally difficult to reconcile, but certain aspects of his character are clear. He was flamboyant and ambitious. He was habitually aggressive and reckless. He was fearless in battle. He was notorious for stretching his superiors' orders, taking risks and, through skill and 'Custer's Luck', succeeding against improbable odds.

During the American Civil War Custer rose from second lieutenant, fresh out of West Point, to the rank of brevet major-general, the youngest in American history. As commander of the famed Wolverines of the Michigan Cavalry Brigade, and of the 3rd Cavalry Division, he was admired by his enemies and friends alike. His Civil War successes confirmed his ability as a competent horse soldier. General Sheridan became his mentor, and repeatedly picked him for critical missions.

After the Civil War, Custer became the commander of the newly formed 7th US Cavalry Regiment. He proved to be a brutal disciplinarian, bringing the 7th under control and gaining many enemies in the process. However, he also had a following of officers who respected and idolised him.

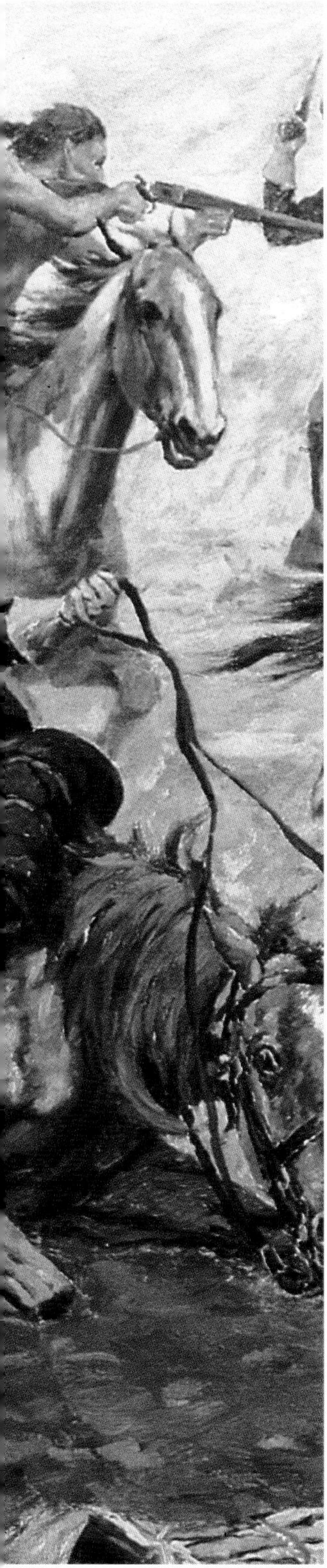

It was for offences during the 1867 Southern Cheyenne campaign in Kansas that Custer had been court martialled. He was charged and convicted on several counts, including absenting himself from his command and ordering deserters shot without trial, and was suspended from rank and command without pay for one year.

Sheridan recalled Custer to command the 7th for the 1868 winter campaign against the Southern Cheyenne. Moving independently, they attacked, surprised and massacred a Cheyenne camp in the snowy Oklahoma wilderness – the Battle of the Washita. Custer had divided his 720-man regiment into four equal parts and surrounded the village at dawn. There were no more than 150 Cheyenne warriors in the camp, and cavalry losses were light. The troopers burned the camp and supplies and shot the ponies. They then withdrew under the cover of darkness as hundreds of warriors attacked from numerous other undetected camps nearby.

The battle was heralded as a victory. It had carried the fight to the Indians in their winter quarters, forcing them to negotiate and eventually accept a treaty. Custer had salvaged his reputation, and he countered criticism that he had massacred 'peaceable Indians' by producing evidence of white captives and raids on white settlements.

Custer believed that the Indians were committed to guerrilla tactics, that they were most vulnerable when attacked in their camps, and were most likely to flee rather than fight a pitched battle with a significant force of federal troops.

On the eve of the 1876 campaign, Custer was again at the centre of a controversy. Custer was originally intended to lead the Dakota Column, but he had testified during Congressional investigations and embarrassed the President, Ulysses S. Grant, who in response had relieved Custer of his command. Generals Sherman and Sheridan intervened on his behalf, and he was allowed to return, but only as commander of the 7th US Cavalry Regiment under the field leadership of General Terry.

FRAGMENTED COMMAND

The officer ranks of the 7th Cavalry were composed of several competent and capable leaders in one of the most petty and bizarre command climates on record. There have been accusations and speculations of alcoholism, cowardice, favouritism and questionable fraternisation between officers. Custer is reported to have kept strict control, but the personality quirks and conflicts evident are extreme.

LEFT Washita Raid *by Charles Schreyvogel. Much of Custer's Indian fighting reputation stemmed from the controversial Battle of the Washita, November 1867. Custer, moving independently with the 7th, surprised and massacred a Cheyenne camp in the snowy Oklahoma wilderness. There were no more than 150 Cheyenne warriors in the camp, and Custer's losses were light. Custer withdrew under the cover of darkness as warriors arrived from numerous other unscouted camps nearby. The Washita raid had carried the fight to the Indians in their winter quarters, forcing them to negotiate and accept a treaty.*

Above *President Ulysses S. Grant took great offence to Custer's testimony during Congressional investigations and relieved him of his command. Generals Sherman and Sheridan eventually convinced Grant to reinstate Custer, in time for the Little Big Horn campaign, on condition that Terry would lead. (U.S. National Archives)*

Above *Last in his class, Custer graduated just in time to participate in the 1st Battle of Mannassas. During the American Civil War, Custer's rise from 2nd lieutenant to the rank of Major General (Brevet) was nothing less than phenomenal. (U.S. Military Academy)*

His second in command, Major Marcus Reno, was a decorated veteran of the Civil War, but this was his first campaign of Indian fighting. He was a comparative newcomer to the regiment, and few of the other officers respected him. He led the regiment during Custer's absence, and that the two trusted each other little. Before President Grant allowed Custer's return, Reno had petitioned Terry for command of the entire expedition.

Captain Frederick Benteen was the regiment's senior company commander and personally commanded H Company. Benteen was a Civil War cavalry commander of some distinction and a skilled Indian fighter. He had fought beside Custer at the Washita, and frequently expressed contempt for Custer's actions there.

Capt. Miles Moylan commanded A Company, part of Reno's battalion. Capt. Thomas M. McDougal commanded B Company and escorted the pack train. Capt. Thomas W. Custer was the C Company commander, and George Custer's younger brother. Capt. Thomas B. Wier, an experienced but often impetuous leader, commanded D Company. Extremely loyal to Custer, he held much contempt for Reno and a deep mistrust distrust of Benteen. 1st Lt. Algernon E. Smith was the E Company, 'Gray Horse Troop', commander. Captain George W. Yates was the F Company commander, and Custer's prefered choice of left wing commander. 1st Lt. Donald McIntosh was the

Captain Frederick W. Benteen was a distinguished Civil War commander and experienced Indian fighter. He was the regiment's senior company commander, and had fought beside Custer at the Washita. Notorious for his displays of contempt for Custer, Benteen apparently had a no-nonsense approach to military leadership that frequently brought the two men into conflict. (Little Big Horn Battlefield National Monument)

1st. Lt. William W. Cooke was Custer's 30-year-old adjutant and one of his finest soldiers. He penned the now famous note for Benteen to 'Come Quick!' Born in Canada, Cooke was a Civil War veteran, and led Custer's sharpshooter detachment at the Washita in 1868.

Major Reno, 1876. He was second in command of the 7th Cavalry and a decorated Civil War veteran, but this was his first campaign of Indian fighting. He led the 7th Cavalry Regiment during Custer's absence, and even petitioned Terry for command of the entire expedition. Terry chose him, to Custer's contempt, to lead a reconnaissance into the Powder and Tongue valleys. Reno violated his instructions, but did confirm the Indian movement toward the Little Big Horn Valley. (Little Big Horn Battlefield National Monument)

G Company commander in Reno's battalion. Captain Miles W. Keogh commanded I Company. He was Custer's right wing commander. 1st Lt. Edward S. Godfrey commanded K Company under Benteen. 1st Lt. James Calhoun, Company L commander, was Custer's brother-in-law. Capt. Thomas H. French was M Company commander under Reno. 2nd Lt. Charles A. Varnum was Custer's experienced and highly competent chief of scouts. 1st Lt. William W. Cooke was Custer's 30-year-old adjutant.

This corporal from the 7th Cavalry is typical of the appearance of the Indian-fighting cavalry in the field. He has removed his blouse which is tied to the saddle and wears only the issue grey flannel shirt. He wears a privately purchased belt with large loops for carbine ammunition and an extra length for pistol ammunition. (Illustration by G. A. Embleton)

Gall was a 36-year-old Hunkpapa Sioux war chief. He grew up as an orphan in the tribe, distinguished himself as a warrior, and Sitting Bull adopted him as a brother. Always leading by example, Gall acted as the principle war chief during the Battle of the Little Big Horn. (U.S. National Archives)

WARRIORS AND WAR CHIEFS

The principal Indian personalities included many of the greatest warriors in Native American history. The foremost leader was Hunkpapa Sioux Chief Sitting Bull. By 1876 he was about 45 years old, and primarily the religious and spiritual master of the defiant Sioux. As a young warrior he had been an influential member of the Brave Hearts akicita (warrior society) and had a reputable war record. He limped, from a bullet wound received in 1856 when he had dispatched a Crow chief in individual combat. Sitting Bull also reportedly belonged to the Kit-Fox akicita. He was considered too old to fight by 1876.

Crazy Horse was about 35 years old in 1876. He was the most celebrated indian combatant of the Sioux Wars, and war chief of a large faction of Oglala extremists. He fiercely contested white expansion, and along with Sitting Bull was a cult leader to the Plains Indians. Crazy Horse had been involved in fighting the Army since before Red Cloud's War. He had learned much and by 1876 he was teaching Sioux and Cheyenne warriors

Crazy Horse, belligerent, contentious, and an accomplished combat leader, the most celebrated war chief of the Little Big Horn campaign. He fiercely contested white expansion, and along with Sitting Bull was a cult leader of the Plains Indians. (S. J. Morrow)

effective tactics for fighting the soldiers.

There were many highly respected warriors and war chiefs who were willing, for this short while, to follow Sitting Bull. Leaders amongst the 120 lodges in the Northern Cheyenne circle included, Lame White Man, Two Moon, a prominent war chief, and Old Bear. Along with Crazy Horse were several renowned Oglala war chiefs, American Horse, Low Dog, war chief since a young teenager, and He-Dog. The Oglala Circle was the largest, with over 240 lodges.

The principal war chief of Sitting Bull's Hunkpapa circle (235 lodges) was Gall, Sitting Bull's 36-year-old adopted brother. Others were Crow-King and Rain in the Face, veteran leader of the Fetterman Fight and Red Cloud's War. About 25 Yanktonnais-Santee Sioux lodges, under Red-on-Top, were also combined with the Hunkpapas. Spotted Eagle was chief of the Sans-Arc Sioux (110 lodges) – staunch supporters of Sitting Bull.

The Blackfoot, led by Jumping Bear and Kill Eagle, the Brule, led by Crow Dog, and Two Kettle Sioux were combined into a circle of about 120 lodges. Red Horse led the Miniconjou circle of about 150 lodges.

Little Powder and his war party of Arapaho braves joined the fight after being initially 'disarmed and detained'. Little Powder's band was one of many rival factions within the camp. The Arapaho did not frequently join with the Sioux and Cheyenne, but they too were in awe of Sitting Bull's spiritual magnetism. All were united by their zeal to fight. The enthusiasm was contagious. Word of these great leaders and their 'medicine' spread throughout the Unceded Territory and the reservations. Young warriors flocked to follow them. Some even left their families on the reservations under government Agency care.

THE OPPOSING ARMIES

THE INDIANS

The culture, society and religion of the Plains Indians was contingent to one thing, personal combat. This defined the very nature of life for the red and the white man on the Great Plains. The white settlers, traders and miners were forced to protect themselves or go elsewhere, and the Army was forced to adapt. The Indian rules of warfare were far more complex than those of the white soldiers. They held standards and practices of personal bravery and tribal honour that were unknown to most professional Army soldiers.

ABOVE *Low Dog reportedly became an Oglala Sioux war chief as a young teenager. A leader in one of the more ferocious warrior societies, he was a powerful and influential Sitting Bull supporter.*

LEFT *Comes Out Holy, Oglala Sioux war chief who followed Gall. This photo, taken at the 1904 world's fair, shows him in long-johns and a traditional 'wild west' show costume. (Michael Her Many Horses)*

The traditional image of the Cheyenne brave. He is equipped with a tomahawk, a cased bow and a quiver of arrows. The buffalo-hide shield is decorated with eagle feathers.

The greatest tool, and the focal point for all warfare in their society, had been donated by the white man some centuries before – the horse. The methods and motives of warfare had become inextricably tied to the skilled use, ownership and tactical mobility of the small, hardy and enduring Indian pony. Riding skills were imperative for fighting and essential for buffalo hunting. Even the immobility of the tribe and its vulnerability in the winter months resulted from limited grazing for their ponies.

The dependence on horses made the camps completely mobile. At the first sign of danger the non-combatants could go through the 'drill' of rapidly packing all essentials and valuables and fleeing, while the warriors took the nearest pony and defended the camp.

WARRIOR SOCIETIES

Within the overall warlike culture of the Great Plains tribes were the elitist akicitas, which cut across tribal distinctions. Each had its own creed, code and level of elitism. Warriors were selectively voted to membership once they had performed certain feats. Some akicitas, such as the Dog-Soldiers, were noted for unyielding tenacity and obstinacy in individual combat. With their distinctive costumes, dances and chants, the akicitas served a purpose in war to instil discipline in the warriors. They also competed against one another for the greater honours of combat. At times, during major raids, the Dog-Soldier akicita served as a police force. More mature and seasoned braves kept the younger or more impetuous warriors from riding ahead of the war band and spoiling a surprise attack or compromising an ambush.

INDIAN TACTICS

The very culture that generated this expertise at combat also dictated collective weaknesses. Warfare for the Plains Indian was a way of life, but it was considered highly spiritual, and strictly individual. They needed no orders to engage, and indeed did not acknowledge orders. This often led to gross lapses in reconnaissance and security. Warriors were not compelled to follow anyone on or off the battlefield. They practised a code of behaviour that rated each act of bravery in battle. Soldiers thought the Indians cowardly for fleeing so frequently and effectively, but in the warrior's culture, it would be no more cowardly than a boxer dodging a right hook.

By 1876 the Sioux and Northern Cheyenne had been warring with the Army for some time, and both were forced to adapt. Most Indians recognised that the soldiers' focus in battle was on killing the enemy and destroying their resources; the soldiers waged total war. Eventually some, such as Crazy Horse, began to encourage a change in method. The tactics of fighting the soldiers gradually became more aggressive as the Indian became better armed, his life and home more seriously threatened.

The principal offensive tactic used against the soldiers was dependent on mounted mobility. It was without design or plan, and involved the summoning of a leader's personal following, which then attracted other

Crow Dog, Brule Sioux chief, an influential leader in tribal politics and combat. He reportedly killed the Brule chief Spotted Tail in 1881. (Nebraska State Historical Society)

Jumping Bear (a.k.a. John Grass), a war chief, along with Kill Eagle, of the bands of Blackfoot allied with Sitting Bull. (Little Big Horn Battlefield National Monument)

individual warriors on the battlefield. A feathered war bonnet served as a rallying point, but a respected warrior such as Crazy Horse was readily recognised and followed. Once there was an assemblage the leader could take some tactical initiative. Put simply, the tactical pattern developed was encirclement, followed by infiltration, sniping and pursuit. The group actions are accentuated by individual acts of bravery such as coup counting, riding in front of the enemy, and riding through his lines. Collective activities include burning grass, stampeding horses, and attempting to lure small bands into an ambush.

INDIAN WEAPONRY

Indian armament gradually improved over the course of the Sioux Wars. After Red Cloud's War, and expansion of the Agencies, Indian access to traders escalated. Those that hunted well in the summer and gathered ponies had much to trade for weapons and ammunition. The government

The average 7th Cavalry trooper on campaign carried many modified or non-issue items. Clockwise from top left: a coffee pot was considered essential; overcoat, rolled and tied to saddle; straw hat, to replace Army issue black felt campaign hat; haversack; tin cup and canteen; cartridge box; carbine sling, adjusted so that a soldier could drop his carbine and draw his pistol at close quarters; model 1872 Cavalry sabre and scabbard, civilian shirt; poncho; sky-blue kersey trousers with seat and inside legs reinforced with canvas.(National Infantry Museum, USA)

Agencies and traders denied responsibility for the increased sophistication of Indian firearms, but modern repeaters abounded.

At the Little Big Horn battle Sioux and Cheyenne warriors were armed with over 30 different types of firearms. Rifles and pistols were objects of great prestige for warriors, but they were considered the least honourable tool for combat. In addition to edged or blunt hand-to-hand weapons, most warriors carried a bow and some a lance.

Archaeology from the Custer battlefield documents the use of everything from muzzle loaders and pistols to modern repeaters such as .44 calibre Henry and Winchester rifles. The repeaters and revolvers were ideal for mounted skirmishing. The ratio of firearms was very high, probably one in three. With an estimated 2,000 warriors, archaeological data suggests 200 or more repeaters and over twice as many other cartridge fired weapons. This does not include Indian capture and use of Army .45 Calibre Springfield Carbines.

CAVALRY TACTICS

Often overlooked in accounts of the Battle of the Little Big Horn are the use of standard cavalry tactics during the engagement. By 1876 the US Army, and especially Custer's 7th Cavalry Regiment, operated under the 1874 manual of Unites States Army Cavalry Tactics by Emory Upton.

The basic unit of troopers was a squad of four mounted men who would not deploy independently. The smallest tactical manoeuvre element was a platoon. There were normally two platoons to a company of 60 troopers. At the Little Big Horn the understrength companies (38-44 men) probably

Scale model of the steamer Far West. *With two levels of open decks, cargo hoists and a very shallow draft, it was able to navigate the Yellowstone and Big Horn rivers. The steamer was a critical logistical asset to the operation, and evacuated 52 wounded troopers from the 7th Cavalry. (J. Thompson)*

consolidated into one large platoon. The 12 companies of the regiment were grouped into battalions. Each battalion had between two and seven companies, which were deployed and numbered in the order of their commanders' seniority. Custer was to employ a standard regimental task organisation in the battle: two battalions of three companies (Reno and Benteen) and one of five companies (his own). Battalions were further divided into two wings, left (even-numbered companies) and right (odd-numbered companies). This ensured that whatever task organisation was applied the commanders immediately knew their position in the formation, and the two senior company commanders became wing commanders.

Skirmish drill was the primary tactic used to engage the enemy. The mounted charge was, on occasion, attempted when surprising a village or seizing key terrain, but it proved ineffective against the more mobile Plains warriors.

Skirmishers were simply a line of troopers spread about five yards apart, deployed to engage the enemy by firepower. It was used to deploy the various battalions and companies from massed column and line formations into the dispersed skirmish line, and could be mounted or dismounted skirmishing. At the Little Big Horn battle the 7th Cavalry maintained a strict adherence to the cavalry doctrine of the day.

The competent employment of Upton's conventional tactics was not enough to defeat the hostile Sioux and Cheyenne. Rarely were warriors aggressive enough to mass or move in an offensive manner. There were some incidents of massed warriors, such as the Fetterman and Wagon Box battles, but these were the exception, and exclusively against small elements. Aggressive behaviour was normally dependent on a tactical superiority against isolated detachments. Warriors would defend their camps, but this usually occurred as an initial flight to protect the non-combatants, followed by a counter attack by infiltration and sniping. One technique advocated and practised by Custer was to seize the pony herd and, if possible, take hostage the non-combatants so that the elusive warriors were forced to counter attack or accept defeat.

The idealised 'Hollywood' image of the horse soldier on the Great Plains. This is another example of myth handed down as reality. In fact more often than not a Cavalry unit on campaign would have had a distinctly rough and ragged appearance. (Eulich Collection)

LOGISTICS

A normal expedition on campaign included a huge logistical tail of several hundred wagons, civilian packers, thousands of horses and mules, and tons of fodder, food and ammunition. In a column of fours, the wagon train would extend half a mile. When a cavalry unit moved to strike independently they stripped down to bare essentials, carrying limited rations, ammunition and fodder on a train of pack mules. The 7th Cavalry needed over 175 mules to carry 15 days supplies. Use of a pack train was the most mobile logistical method, but it was still slow and unwieldy. It was also of limited duration, a pack mule would eat all the grain he could carry in 20 days, and could not survive on prairie grass like the Indian pony.

The scout element played a significant role in tracking and engaging the Indians. Custer's Indian scout detachment, led by Lt. Varnum, provided him with navigation, terrain knowledge and intelligence on the enemy's location, size and disposition. The Indian scouts were not expected to fight, though some of the more loyal ones did.

CAVALRY WEAPONRY

Troopers of the 7th Cavalry carried two standard firearms; the breech-loaded .45/55 calibre Springfield Carbine (Model 1873) and the .45 calibre Colt single action revolver (Model 1873). Both were very effective. At the Little Big Horn fight each trooper was issued 100 rounds of carbine ammunition, half of it in his cartridge belt and half in his saddlebags, and 24 rounds of pistol ammunition.

The Springfield has been blamed for Custer's defeat, due to its single shot capability and alleged jamming. This is simply untrue. Archaeological evidence of spent cartridges indicates a minute percentage of 'pried' brass casings. Also, the weapons proved more than adequate for the defence of Reno Hill. While the repeating rifles had double the Springfield's rate of fire, they had less than half the effective range. Several of the officers and civilians carried their own weapons. Custer used a Remington sporting rifle and two snub-nosed Irish constabulary pistols. The Indian Scouts were normally armed with the Army Springfield Carbine. Custer had ordered the 7th Cavalry to box their sabres before departing on this campaign.

TERRY AND GIBBON

GIBBON'S ENCOUNTERS

'... movement is started against a Sioux village which has been discovered on [the] Tongue River, but on account of having been discovered before the crossing is completed, and the difficulty of making the horses swim the river, the movement is abandoned.'

LT. EDWARD J. MCCLERNAND, MONTANA COLUMN, 17 MAY 1876

Colonel John Gibbon commanded what is referred to as the Montana Column. He had been in the field since his 1 April departure from Fort Ellis, Montana. His column included four companies of the 2nd Cavalry Regiment and five companies of the 7th Infantry Regiment (450 soldiers in all). On orders from Terry, Gibbon halted his movement eastward along the Yellowstone and remained in camp at the mouth of Tullock Creek from 21 April to 9 May.

While Gibbon was stationary along the northern boundary of the Unceded Territory, the Sioux and Cheyenne were active. By 8 April Crazy Horse's Oglala and Northern Cheyenne winter roamers had consolidated with Sitting Bull's camp near Chalk Butte. This was far to the east of Gibbon, but a westward movement had begun. By 20 April the Sans Arc under Spotted Eagle had joined with the main camp at the head of Sheep Creek. Word of Crook's Powder River attack had spread rapidly amongst the villages.

The first sign of new grass for the Indian ponies came with warmer weather, about 22 April. The Santee Sioux with Chief Red-on-Top and other Cheyenne joined with the large camp on the Powder River at the Mizpah around 26 April. Within a few days new grass was everywhere. The ponies could graze as the camps moved farther and faster. The camp was at the mouth of Pumpkin Creek on the Tongue River by 5 May, when the Blackfoot Sioux under Kill Eagle arrived.

While Gibbon was camped at the mouth of Tullock Creek he sent several reconnaissance patrols, but could only confirm where the Sioux were not. On 3 May, by which time Gibbon thought the Sioux might have returned to the reservation, the hostiles found Gibbon, and there followed three weeks of continuous, but unchallenged, harassment of Gibbon's Montana Column.

The Montana column under Colonel John Gibbon, 7th Infantry, unsuccessfully patrolled the Yellowstone River from April until 21 June, when he joined forces with Gen. Terry. The latter had intended to remain on the steamer Far West *and have Gibbon lead his column toward the Little Big Horn Valley from the north, but Gibbon fell sick. (U.S. National Archives)*

MONTANA COLUMN

COL. JOHN GIBBONS

Adjutant: *1st Lt. Levi F. Burnett,* (7th Infantry)
Quartermaster: *1st Lt. Joshua W. Jacobs,* (7th Infantry)
Engineer Officer: *2nd Lt. Edward J. McClernand*

Crow Indian Scouts and Mounted Detachment, 7th Inf. *(1st Lt. James H. Bradley)*
25 Enlisted Indian Scouts *(Crows)*
1 Officer, 12 Men

Gatling Gun Detachment, 7th Inf.
(2nd Lt Charles A. Woodruff)
1 Officer, 6 Men)

Capt. Freeman's Battalion, 7th Inf.
Company A, 7th Infantry:
Capt. William Logan
2 Officers, 23 Men
Company B, 7th Infantry:
Capt. Thaddeus S. Kirtland
2 Officers, 31 Men
Company E, 7th Infantry:
Capt. Walter Clifford
2 Officers, 35 Men
Company H, 7th Infantry:
Capt. Henry B. Freeman
2 Officers, 36 Men
Company I, 7th Infantry:
1st Lt. William L. English
2 Officers, 31 Men
Company K, 7th Infantry:
Capt. James M. Sanno
2 Officers, 18 Men

2nd Cavalry *(Maj. James S. Brisbin)*
2nd Lt. Charles B. Schofield,
Adjutant Assistant Surgeon: *1st Lt. Holmes O. Paulding*

Company F, 2nd Cavalry
(2nd Lt. Charles F. Roe)
1 Officer, 45 Men
Company G, 2nd Cavalry
(Capt. Nicholas Wheelan)
2 Officers, 34 Men
Company H, 2nd Cavalry
(Capt. Edward Ball)
2 Officers, 41 Men
Company L, 2nd Cavalry
(Capt. Lewis Thompson)
2 Officers, 37 Men

Gibbon failed to give Terry an accurate report on the enemy situation. His personal account referred to the area as 'Indian infested', but on 27 May he sent a dispatch to Terry downplaying any significant activity. Gibbon acknowledged war parties, but said 'no camps have been seen'. He did request the use of a steamboat for 'passing troops across the river'.

TERRY'S ADVANCE

The Dakota Column, with Terry in command, had departed Fort Abraham Lincoln on 17 May and was moving steadily west. The column included the 12 companies of the 7th Cavalry Regiment, commanded by Custer, five infantry companies, three Gatling guns, 39 Indian scouts, over 150 wagons and 200 teamsters. The column made very slow progress (only 165 miles in 13 days). On 29 May, while the main column camped, Custer took four companies of the 7th Cavalry on a limited scout. He found no sign of the hostile tribes.

On 31 May, Terry chastised Custer for departing the command. After crossing the Little Missouri River, the immense column had taken the wrong trail in Custer's absence. The Dakota Column continued west, halted on 1 and 2 June for a snowstorm, then covered 25 miles on 3 June, and received Gibbon's 27 May dispatch as they neared the Yellowstone.

DAKOTA COLUMN

BRIG.GEN. ALFRED H. TERRY

Adjutant: *Capt. Edward W. Smith,* USA (18th Infantry)
Engineer Officer: *1st Lt. Edward Maguire,* Engineer Corps
Quartermaster (acting): *1st Lt. Henry J. Nolan* (7th Cavalry)
Commisary of Substinance (acting): *2nd Lt. Richard E. Thompson* (6th Infantry)
Ordinance Officer: *Capt. Ortho E. Maguire,* Ordinance Corps
Chief Medical Officer: *Capt. John W. Williams,* Assisstant Surgeon
ADC: *Capt. Robert P. Hughes,* (3rd Infantry)
ADC: *1st Lt. Eugene B. Gibbs* (6th Infantry)

Steamer *Far West*
(Capt. Grant Marsh)
Company B, 6th Infantry,
(Capt. Steven Barker)[1]
2 Officers, 44 Men

Steamer *Josephine*
(Capt. Mart Coulson)
Escort Detachment, Co. C, D & I, 6th Inf., *(1st Lt. Frederick W. Thibault)*
1 Officer, 17 Men

6th Infantry,
(Major Orlando H. Moore)
Co. D, 6th Inf.
(Capt. Daniel H. Murdock)
1 Officer, 32 Men
Co. I, 6th Inf.
(2nd Lt. George B. Walker)
1 Officer, 35 Men
Gatling Gun Battery, 20th Inf. Detachment *(2nd Lt. William H. Low)*
3 Caisson-drawn Gatling Guns
2 Officers, 23 Men
Co. C, 17th Inf.
(Capt. Malcomb McArthur)[2]
3 Officers, 44 Men
Co. G, 17th Inf.,
(Capt. Louis H. Sanger)[3]
3 Officers, 45 Men

7th Cavalry, *(Lt.Col. George A. Custer)*
(See 7th Cavalry Order of Battle)

NOTES
1 Terry's Escort, attached to Steamer
2 Attached to 6th Inf. on 12 June
3 Attached to 6th Inf. on 12 June

Terry arranged for supplies from the steamers *Josephine* and *Far West* at the Yellowstone/Glendive Creek depot to be pushed forward to the mouth of the Powder River. The Dakota Column pushed on toward the Powder River, 90 miles ahead. Terry sent couriers to Gibbon, but none reached him. Terry rode ahead, leaving Custer in charge of the column. At the Powder River depot Terry found the Steamer *Far West* and elements of Gibbon's Montana Column, led by Major James S. Brisbin, 2nd Cavalry, and learned of the hostiles' concentration and suspected location. Terry rode the *Far West* up the Yellowstone River until he found Gibbon. By 8 June Terry had effective command of both columns, but the main hostile camps had moved south along the Rosebud Valley, towards Crook.

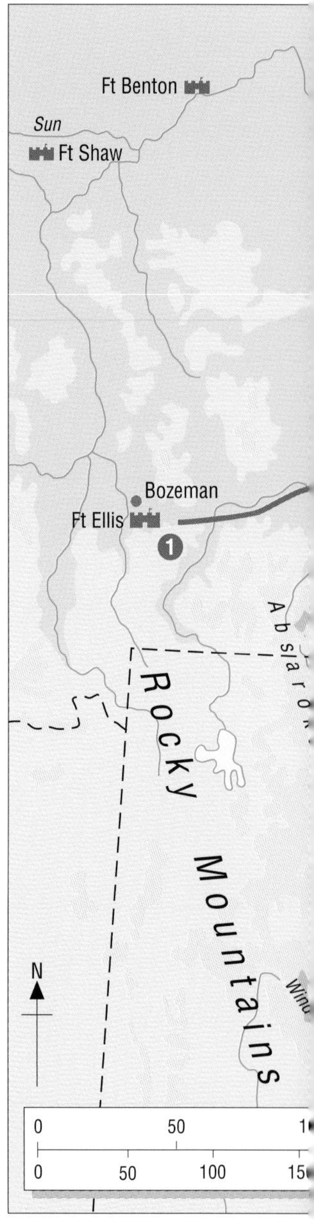

CROOK'S REPULSE

'So closely did the Indians approach our skirmishers at times that they inflicted several wounds from battle axes, lances and arrows, and in one or two instances they closed in upon a brave soldier and got his scalp before comrades could rush forward to the rescue.'

CORRESPONDENT ROBERT E. STRAHORN, BATTLE OF THE ROSEBUD, 17 JUNE 1876

The hostile Sioux and Cheyenne participated in their annual Sun Dance, around 5 June on the Rosebud River. During the spiritual ritual, Sitting Bull sacrificed 50 pieces of flesh and fell into a trance. When he regained consciousness, he prophesied that he had seen many white soldiers falling upside-down into their large village to be killed. This was accepted as prediction of a great victory over the 'Long Knives'. The camp moved south and continued to grow as word spread among the tibes of Sitting Bull's 'medicine'.

FEDERAL ADVANCE, APRIL-JUNE 1876

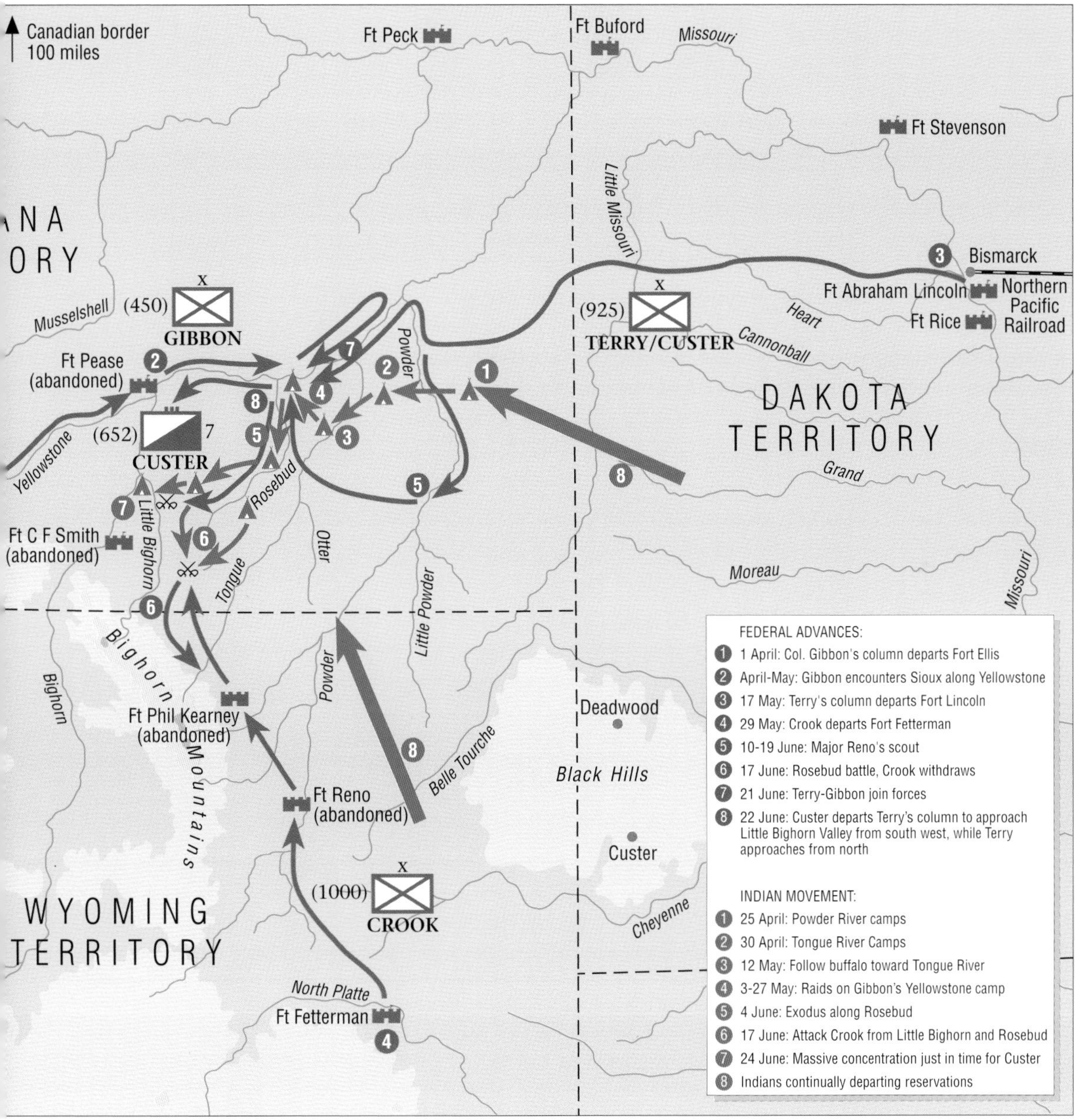

On 9 June warriors departed from the camp on Muddy Creek and raided Crook's Tongue River depot. Crook had been on the move since 29 May with over 1,000 men. By 11 June he had established a permanent supply camp on Goose Creek (now Sheridan, Wyoming). His attack force, augmented with over 80 armed civilians and 260 Crow and Shoshone allies, departed from the Goose Creek camp on 16 June. This movement was monitored by a band of warriors led by the Cheyenne Little Hawk, who quickly reported the news of the approaching soldiers to the main congregation of hostiles, now camped on Reno Creek.

During a spirited inter-tribal council meeting, the anxious young war chiefs decided on a spoiling attack to surprise Crook on the march. On the morning of 17 June, Crook's force was on the move by 3.00 am but halted after sunrise along a bend in the Rosebud Creek to rest the animals and make coffee. At 8.30 am hundreds of Sioux and Cheyenne warriors, under the field leadership of Crazy Horse, attacked, sweeping in from the north across the rolling hills and steep ravines. The column was initially surprised, but with the help of the Indian allies, managed to fight them to a stalemate.

The Battle of The Rosebud concluded with the warriors breaking contact and returning to their village. There were ten soldiers killed and 21 wounded. Indian casualties are estimated at less than 100. Crook had been unprepared for the Indians' aggressiveness, or such numbers. On 18 June his entire column returned to the Goose Creek Camp to await reinforcements. This withdrawal removed his significant force from the field for over seven weeks. With the climax of the Sioux War at hand, the Department of the Platte, and nearly half of the theatre's combat power was effectively out of the campaign.

The southern column, led by General George Crook was surprised and attacked on 17 June by Sitting Bull's warriors under the field leadership of Crazy Horse. Crook was unprepared for the Indians' aggressiveness, but, with the help of Crow and Shoshone Indian allies, managed to fight them to a stalemate. The Battle of the Rosebud concluded with Crook's entire column withdrawing to await reinforcements. (U.S. National Archives)

RENO'S SCOUT

'I can tell you where the Indians are not, and much more information when I see you in the morning.' Major Marcus Reno, 19 June 1876

While Crook was conducting the Rosebud campaign, his second expedition of the year, Terry was continuing his search for the hostiles. Terry departed his camp near the Powder River depot on 10 June and moved west along the southern bank of the Yellowstone River. Before the column's advance, Terry ordered Major Reno to conduct a reconnaissance with Mitch Boyer as guide, several Arikara Indian scouts, six companies from Custer's 7th Cavalry (B, C, E, F, I and L), a Gatling gun and 100 pack mules.

When Terry selected Reno to command the scouting detachment, Custer was furious. He protested, surprised that Terry would detach half of his regimental command and not allow him to lead it. Terry didn't change his mind. Some accounts speculate that Terry intended to use the limited scout to exercise his authority over the ever insubordinate Custer. Others point out that Terry needed Custer with him to keep the rest of the Dakota column on track. Custer had indeed been instrumental as the key pathfinder and orchestrator of the scouts and guides.

RIGHT *One of three Gatling guns General Terry had with his command. Recognising the size and weight of these virtual artillery pieces, and the rough terrain to be traversed is essential in understanding why Custer would not, and could not, include them on his march. (Little Big Horn Battlefield National Monument)*

On 25 June Reno commanded a battalion of three companies – A, G, and M – and then assumed command of the hilltop defence. After the Little Big Horn disaster Reno requested an official inquiry. The Board, which convened in 1879, exonerated him of punishable negligence. Reno was later court martialled on other unrelated charges and discharged.

Reno was directed to travel in a clockwise loop, south along the Powder River and back north along the Mizpah and Pumpkin creeks. Reno found little sign of the hostiles, so he deviated to investigate the camp diverted that had been reported in May by Bradley, 20 miles west on the Tongue River.

Once at the Tongue River village Reno and scout Mitch Boyer counted over 400 lodge sites. The Arikara Indian scouts also located an immense trail leading west toward the Rosebud Valley. He disobeyed his instructions and followed the trail. When he found signs of more recent camps along Rosebud Creek, Reno put his troopers into a 'patrol base' and sent the scouts to follow the trail. They went about 20 miles, until they were a day behind the hostiles, before they turned back. Reno had, by his own initiative, confirmed the direction and distance of the main Indian camp. The hostiles were moving south, up the Rosebud, and most likely would cross over to the Little Big Horn River.

On 19 June Reno's detachment returned to the Yellowstone and linked up with Terry near the mouth of the Tongue. Reno's reconnaissance had been an operational success. Terry was very satisfied with the information, but both he and Custer were angry over Reno's disobedience.

Premonition *by Don Stives depicts the 7th Cavalry at the Little Heart River on the morning of 18 May 1876, as Lt.Col. George Custer bids his wife Libby farewell. It was the last time she would see him. On 6 July 1876 she would be notified of the death of her husband, his brothers Tom and Boston Custer, nephew Harry Armstrong Reed and her sister's husband Lt. James Calhoun – all killed in the Battle of the Little Big Horn.*

FAR W

TERRY'S PLAN

'I have had but little experience in Indian fighting, and Custer has had much, and he is sure he can whip anything he meets.'
GENERAL ALFRED TERRY, 21 JUNE 1876

On 21 June 1876 Terry held a strategy conference aboard the steamer *Far West*. He issued to all of the commanders his orders for offensive operations against the Sioux and Cheyenne hostiles thought to be in the Little Big Horn Valley. The primary focus was on bringing the hostiles to battle, and finding and engaging the largest concentration possible was the highest priority.

Terry's plan was to release Custer and his 7th Cavalry Regiment to move independently as a mobile strike force, approaching the Little Big Horn from the south. With the remainder of infantry and 2nd Cavalry Gibbon would cross the Yellowstone and approach the Little Big Horn Valley from the north, blocking any hostile escape in that direction.

Custer's written instructions were to '... proceed up the Rosebud in pursuit of the Indians whose trail was discovered by Major Reno ... preclude the possibility of the escape of the Indians'. Terry needed time to get the infantry into their blocking position north of the suspected hostiles, so he directed Custer not to follow the trail directly to the Little Big Horn Valley but to 'still proceed southward, perhaps as far as the headwaters of the Tongue, and then turn towards the Little Horn, feeling constantly, however, to your left, so as to preclude the possibility of the escape of the Indians to the south or south-east by passing around your left flank'.

Most noteworthy in Terry's written instructions was the clause virtually allowing Custer a free hand to do as he wanted: '... the Department Commander places too much confidence in your zeal, energy, and ability to wish to impose upon you precise orders which might hamper your action when nearly in contact with the enemy ...'.

Custer was to take with him all 12 companies of his regiment, 15 days supplies on 175 pack mules, his Arikara Indian scouts and six of the best Crow scouts from Lt. Bradley's detachment. This included Mitch Boyer and George Herendeen, which left Terry without a guide. The blocking force would consist of the remaining five companies of the 7th Infantry, three of the Gatling guns, and four companies of the 2nd Cavalry, under Major

The most critical logistical and communication asset to Terry's command was the steamer Far West. *Expertly captained by civilian Grant Marsh, the* Far West *had been chartered by the US Government to support the 1876 campaign. (Little Big Horn Battlefield National Monument)*

The Custer 'clique'. Officers within the unit either clung to Custer or detested him. From left to right are Lt. Nelson Bronson, Lt. George D. Wallace, Lt.Col. George A. Custer, Lt. Benjamin Hodgson, Mrs T. McDougall, Mrs G.A. Custer, Capt. Thomas McDougall, Lt. William Badger, Mrs G. Yates, Capt. George Yates, Charles W. Thompson, Maggie Custer Calhoun, Agnes Bates, Col. J.S. Poland, Lt. Charles Varnum, Lt.Col. William Carlin, 17th Inf., Mrs M. Moylan, Lt. Thomas W. Custer, Capt. William Thompson, Lt.Lt. James Calhoun, Mrs D. McIntosh, Capt. Miles Moylan, Lt. Donald McIntosh. (Little Big Horn Battlefield National Monument)

James S. Brisbin. One company of infantry was assigned as escort for the steamer *Far West*, and one to guard the forward supply base along the Yellowstone.

The Montana Column had ample firepower, but it was much too small and lacked mobility for offensive operations. Terry had already depleted a significant portion of his combat power. A large contingent of his command (five infantry companies and nearly 300 dismounted troopers and civilian employees) had been left far behind at the Powder River depot. Of the 12 infantry companies at Terry's disposal seven would be intentionally excluded from the crucial stages of the operation. Later, the entire Montana Column would also be excluded, but not necessarily by design.

The Montana Column received no written orders, but were to be ferried across the Yellowstone by the *Far West*, to be in position as soon as possible. Terry's written instructions to Custer referred to his intentions. 'The column of Colonel Gibbon is now in motion for the mouth of the Big Horn. As soon as it reaches that point it will cross the Yellowstone and move up at least as far as the forks of the Big and Little Horns. Of course

Custer, his wife Libby and brother Capt. Tom Custer. George Custer was wholly devoted to his wife. Several of Custer's 1867 court martial charges were related to his departure from his regiment when on campaign to see her during a feared epidemic.

its future movements must be controlled by circumstances as they arise, but it is hoped that the Indians, if upon the Little Horn, may be so nearly inclosed by the two columns that their escape will be impossible.' Terry intended to establish his headquarters on the Far West, but when Gibbon fell sick on 23 June and was interned to the steamer, Terry led the blocking force.

Terry, at Brisbin's urging, offered to augment Custer's element with the 2nd Cavalry, but Custer's declined with the reply, 'The 7th can handle anything it meets.'

CUSTER'S INDEPENDENT COMMAND

"Custer is smarting under the rebuke of the President, and wants an independent command, and I wish to give him a chance to do something ."

GENERAL ALFRED TERRY, 21 JUNE 1876 .

At noon on 22 June, Custer and his 7th Cavalry separated from General Terry and the Montana Column. They were travelling light. Custer was planning to march nearly 100 miles over rough terrain and fight an elusive enemy along the way. He halted early the first day, only 12 miles up the Rosebud, and held his own officer's conference that evening. Security was to be heightened now that they were going deeper into Indian territory. The command was to keep consolidated on the march and be prepared for attack at all times. Each man would sleep with his weapon, and the trains would conduct a drill to guard the animals should the alarm be sounded. No bugle calls would be used except in emergency, and gunfire was to be restricted.

The 7th Cavalry moved south at 5.00 am on 23 June, following the Rosebud Creek but remaining on the less restrictive high ground. The Arikaras, managed by 2nd Lt. Varnum, scouted ahead on both sides of the valley. Mitch Boyer and the Crow scouts pushed far ahead and provided Custer with knowledge of the local terrain. Soon the column encountered the large campsites Reno had discovered. At 2.00 pm they passed the point where Reno had halted his pursuit a few days before. The trail of Indian ponies, lodge-pole drag marks and abandoned temporary shelters led to the south. Custer followed.

Custer covered more than 35 miles before nightfall on 23 June, and departed again at 5.00 am on 24 June, soon finding the site of the Sun Dance held several weeks earlier. The enormous Indian pony herd was evident from the close-eaten grass. The scout Herendeen also identified the light-coloured scalp of 2nd Cavalry Trooper Augustus Stoker hanging on display. Stoker had been killed during one of the raids on Gibbon the previous month. Herendeen later noted to Custer the point at which he had been instructed to carry a dispatch to Terry (the reason Herendeen was attached to Custer) but Custer had nothing to report and kept Herendeen with him.

At 1.00 pm, after travelling 20 miles, Custer halted the column while Lt. Varnum and some scouts doubled back to investigate a diverging trail. Custer was greatly concerned, no doubt from his Washita experience, over

2nd Lt. Charles A. Varnum was Custer's experienced and very competent chief of scouts. He continued to provide Custer with intelligence until engaged. He was shot in both legs during the hilltop defence. (U.S. Military Academy)

the threat posed by undetected Indian concentrations. The diverging trail was found to rejoin the main Indian trail and the 7th was moving again by 4.00 pm.

Some time that afternoon the sizeable trail became fresh. It turned up Davis Creek, toward the Little Big Horn Valley. Custer ordered a rest halt near the mouth of the creek and sent his scouts further forward. The fresh trail indicated to Custer that the main hostile camp was very close. What

7TH CAVALRY REGIMENT

(LT.COL. GEORGE A. CUSTER)

HQ/Staff (6 Officers, 2 Enlisted)
Maj. Marcus A. Reno
1st. Lt. William W. Cooke, Adjutant
1st Lt. Edwin Lord, Assistant Surgeon
Dr. James M. DeWolf
Dr. Henry R. Porter
Sgt. Maj. William H. Sharrow
Chief Trumpeter Henry Voss
2 Citizens: Mark Kellogg, and Autie Reed (Custer's nephew)

Indian Scouts Detachment
2nd Lt. Charles A. Varnum,
2nd Lt. Luther R. Hare
2 Officers, 2 Interpreters, 5 guides (quartermaster Employees), 35 Enlisted Indian Scouts

Pack Train Detachment
(1st Lt. Edward G. Mathey)
1 Officer, 6 mule-packers (quartermaster Employees)
Company B
(Capt. Thomas M. McDougal)[1]
1 Officer, 48 Men

RENO'S BATTALION[2]

Maj. Marcus A. Reno,
2nd Lt. Benjamin H Hodgson, Adjutant[3]
Company A (*Capt. Myles Moylan, 1st Lt. Charles C. Derudio, 1st Sgt. William Heyn)*
2 Officers, 48 Men
Company G *(1st Lt. Donald Mcintosh, 2nd Lt. George D. Wallace, (1st Sgt. on leave))*
2 Officers, 43 Men
Company M *(Capt. Thomas H French, 1st Sgt. John M. Ryan)*
1 Officer, 57 Men

BENTEEN'S BATTALION[4]

Capt. Frederick W. Benteen
Company H *(Capt. Frederick W. Benteen, 1st Lt. Francis M. Gibson, 1st Sgt. Joseph McCurry)*
2 Officers, 45 Men
Company D *(Capt. Thomas B. Wier, 2nd Lt. Winfield S. Edgerly, 1st Sgt. Michael Martin)*
2 Officers, 52 Men
Company K *(1st Lt. Edward S. Godfrey, 1st Sgt. Dewitt Winney)*
1 Officer, 41 Men

CUSTER'S BATTALION[5]

Lt.Col. George A. Custer
Company C *(Capt. Thomas W. Custer, 2nd Lt. Henry Harington, 1st Sgt. Edwin Bobo)*
2 Officers, 50 Men
Company E *(1st Lt. Algeron E. Smith, 2nd Lt. James G. Sturgis, 1st Sgt. Fred Hohmeyer)*
2 Officers, 46 Men
Company F *(Capt. George W. Yates, 2nd Lt. William V. Reily, 1st Sgt. Michael Kenny)*
2 Officers, 51 Men
Company I *(Capt. Miles W. Keogh, 1st Lt. James E. Porter, 1st Sgt. Frank E. Varden)*
2 Officers, 46 Men
Company L *(1st Lt. James Calhoun, 2nd Lt. John Crittenden, 1st Sgt. James Butler)*
2 Officers, 57 Men

NOTES
1 Escort to pack-train on 25 June
2 On 25 June an ad hoc Battalion of 3 companies (A, G, and M)
3 Attached on temporary duty from Company B
4 On 25 June an ad hoc Battalion of 3 companies (H, D, and K)
5 On 25 June an ad hoc Battalion of 5 Companies (C, E, F, I, and L)

Brule Village *(Grabill). In the six days following the Rosebud battle, Sitting Bull's village more than doubled in size, from 400 to nearly 1000 lodges, and from 3000 to nearly 7000 people. They had no intention of fleeing, and were anxious to fight. None of the whites foresaw this, Lt.Col. George A. Custer included.*

he didn't know was that the new trail was from the mass exodus of bands from the Missouri River Agencies following Sitting Bull's older trail.

On 19 June, while Reno was reporting the results of his reconnaissance, the hostiles spent six days celebrating the Rosebud battle at their camp near the Little Big Horn River. By 23 June the camp had experienced a great influx of summer roamers. In the six days following the Rosebud battle, the main hostile camp more than doubled its size, to over 1,000 lodges and 7,000 inhabitants. There were an estimated 1,500-2,000 warriors from Northern Cheyenne and five major Sioux tribes. The Indians had no intention of fleeing. They were determined to stand and fight.

By nightfall the 7th had covered 70 miles in two and a half days. The Crows scouted up the Davis Creek. From the summit of the divide between the Rosebud and Big Horn valleys they searched the horizon for a sign of the hostiles. From their vantage point, a promontory called the Crow's Nest, the scouts were looking into the setting sun. They could only confirm that the trail continued on past the divide, and noted a few tepees about eight miles down Reno Creek. Custer received this intelligence around 9.00 pm while bivouacked near the mouth of Davis Creek.

Custer decided to follow the fresh trail, against Terry's instructions to veer further south. Evidently he saw 'sufficient reason for departing from them'. He sent his scouts back to the Crow's Nest to continue observation, and decided to move the regiment closer. Despite three gruelling days of marching behind them, Custer had the 7th Cavalry conduct a night march toward the Little Big Horn. They moved at 11.00 pm, six miles up Davis Creek, getting very spread out and separated. Custer ordered a halt at 2.00 am, five miles short of the divide. When the tired troopers finally bivouacked in the morning hours of 25 June, Custer gave orders to rest in preparation for an assault the following day.

Meanwhile Terry and the Montana Column were making terrible progress. Without adequate local guides, and with Terry's self-admitted tactical ineptness, they became diverted through brutal terrain and were

INDIAN NATIONS

NORTHERN PLAINS, JUNE 1865

SITTING BULL
Chief and Spiritual Leader

Hunkpapa Sioux Circle 260 Lodges
(including 25 Lodges of Yanktonnais and Santee Sioux)10
Gall (Principle War Chief), Crow King (War Chief), Rain-in-the-Face (War Chief), Four Horns (War Chief), Black Moon, Brown Back, Deeds,

Santees Circle 25 Lodges
Inkpaduta (Red-on-Top), Walks-Under-the-Ground

Oglala Sioux (Red Cloud's Tribe) 240 Lodges
Crazy Horse 100 Lodges
American Horse (Chief) 37 Lodghes, Low Dog (War Chief), Little Big Man, He-Dog (War Chief) 10 Lodges, Kicking Bear Jack Red Cloud, Big Road, Walking Blanket Woman

Combined Blackfoot, Brule, and Two Kettle Sioux Circle 120 Lodges
Blackfeet Sioux 34 Lodges
Jumping Bear (War Chief), Kill Eagle, Scabby Face

Two Kettle Sioux 18 Lodges

Brule Sioux 68 Lodges
Brave Bird, Coffee, Crazy Bull, Elk Thunder, Grass Rope, High Bald Eagle, Hollow Horn Eagle,

Miniconjou Sioux Circle 150 Lodges
Red Horse (Miniconjou Chief), Touch the Clouds (7' War Chief), Hump (War Chief), Lame Dear (War Chief), Fast Bull, High Backbone.

Sans Arc Circle 110 Lodges
Spotted Eagle (Sans Arc Chief), Black Eagle (War Chief).

Arapahoe
Left Hand, Waterman, Yellow Eagle, Yellow Fly.

Northern Cheyenne Circle 120 Lodges
War Chiefs: Magpie Eagle 13 Lodges, Dull Knife 12 Lodges, LittleWolf 7 Lodges, Old Bear 40 Lodges, Lame Dear 4 Lodges, Lame White Man, Brave Bear, Two Moon, Dirty Moccasins., Mad Wolf, Calf, Roan Bear, Buffalo Calf Road Woman

Capt. Thomas W. Custer was the C Company commander and George Custer's younger brother. He was a two-time recipient of the Civil War Medal of Honour. During the battle, he most likely served as aide to his brother, with the competent 2nd Lt. Henry Harington directing C Company. (Little Big Horn Battlefield National Monument)

LEFT *Custer's Crow and Arikara scouts received instructions from Custer to drive the Sioux pony herds away and deprive the enemy of their mobility. Indian scouts were not expected to fight once they found the enemy, but were allowed to take spoils – ponies etc – as a reward for their services. (Little Big Horn Battlefield National Monument)*

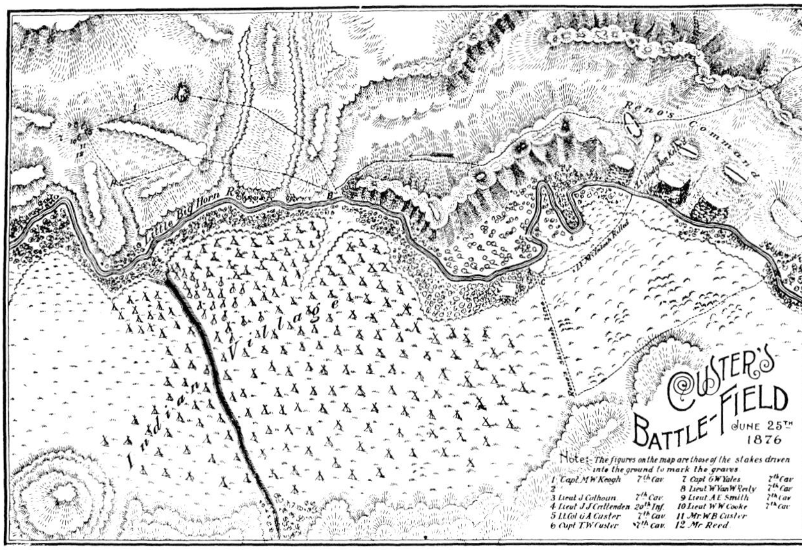

This contemporary map is a useful reference to identify the course of the Little Big Horn River and wooded areas, but other details such as the contour and orientation of Battle Ridge and the Reno-Benteen defence site are inaccurate. The arrows depicting Custer's movement are typical of traditional accounts. (US National Archives)

hopelessly behind schedule. Rather than advancing up Tullock Creek, Terry cut over to the nearly impassable Big Horn Valley. When Custer went into battle, Terry was 40 miles away.

At dawn on 25 June the Indian scouts told Lt. Varnum that they saw smoke on the horizon and a large pony herd, indicating a large Indian camp 15 miles to the north-west. Varnum was unable to confirm this with field glasses, and said as much in his message to Custer. He also noted of two tepees about seven miles away. By 8.45 am Custer was en route to the Crow's Nest to clarify Varnum's report; the regiment continued its march.

From the Crow's Nest at 10.00 am Custer saw nothing through his field glasses, and he openly doubted the presence of a large camp. Custer acknowledged to the Indian scouts that the hostiles could indeed be there, but where and in how many separate camps he could not know. The only hard evidence he held of the enemy camp's size and location was the fresh trail leading toward the Little Big Horn. It indicated that numerous factional tribes were present – a rare alliance, which would mean an eventual separation. Most of the trails indicated non-combatant families, property in tow and an exceptionally large pony herd. This was a vulnerability that Custer could exploit in the attack, and it would slow them down in any pursuit. The Crow scouts said that there were more hostiles than the 7th Cavalry had cartridges. Custer was not concerned with numbers. His chief fear was of an Indian escape.

Before departing the Crow's Nest, Custer's brother Tom brought word of 'discovery' by the Sioux. Two parties of hostiles had spotted the soldiers. The scouts warned Custer that they could not surprise the hostiles now, but he disagreed with them.

Custer told Lt. Varnum and Lt. Godfrey that he didn't really believe the Indians were in the Little Big Horn Valley, but when he called his officers together he reportedly said: '... the largest Indian camp on the North American Continent is ahead ...' He may not have believed it, but he could not have been more right.

THE BATTLE OF THE LITTLE BIGHORN

Capt. Thomas M. McDougal commanded Company B and escorted the pack train. The slow moving packs fell several miles behind during the 7th Cavalry's approach to the Little Big Horn Valley. (BYU Camp Collection)

While Custer was at the Crow's Nest, Major Reno moved the regiment forward to the foot of the incline. Custer received more reports of Indian sightings when he rejoined his men. A party of seven Sioux had been seen briefly on a ridge-line. Custer ordered officers' call. He had made a crucial decision; he was not going to wait until 26 June to engage. Custer expressed to his officers that since 'all hope of surprise was now lost', and to prevent the Indians from fleeing it was necessary to attack at once.

Before departing, Custer organised the regiment into four groups: one battalion, companies D, H and K under Capt. Benteen (120 men), took the lead; a second battalion, companies A, G, and M, was under Major Reno (175 men); Custer led a third battalion with two wings; Captain Yates led companies E and F; and Captain Keogh led companies C, I and L (221 men total). The slow-moving pack train was left to follow with Captain McDougal's B Company, as guards, and seven men from each company detached to keep the mules moving (175 men) and improve the mobility and security of the trains. Varnum was to scout ahead of the main body, and would later be under Reno's control. The 7th Cavalry resumed its advance at 11.45 am.

After crossing the divide, Custer halted the command again. He had developed his plan into a three-pronged movement-to-contact: Custer on the right, Reno in the centre and Benteen on the left. He ordered Benteen south-east to scout and cover the left flank of the advance. His orders to Benteen were for a 'reconnaissance and attack' over a series of ridges that blocked any view in that direction, to report any Indian sightings and to 'pitch into anything' he encountered.

Benteen objected saying, 'Hadn't we better keep the regiment together General? If this is as big a camp as they say, we'll need every man we have.' Custer dismissed his suggestion, sending two supplementary orders for Benteen to continue past the first few ridges should he see nothing.

Custer is often erroneously imputed with adopting a plan similar to his attack in the 1867 Washita battle, dividing his command to attack from different angles. This was not the case. He had no specific target when he organised the regiment, and had no further information when he sent Benteen to the left.

7TH CAVALRY APPROACH

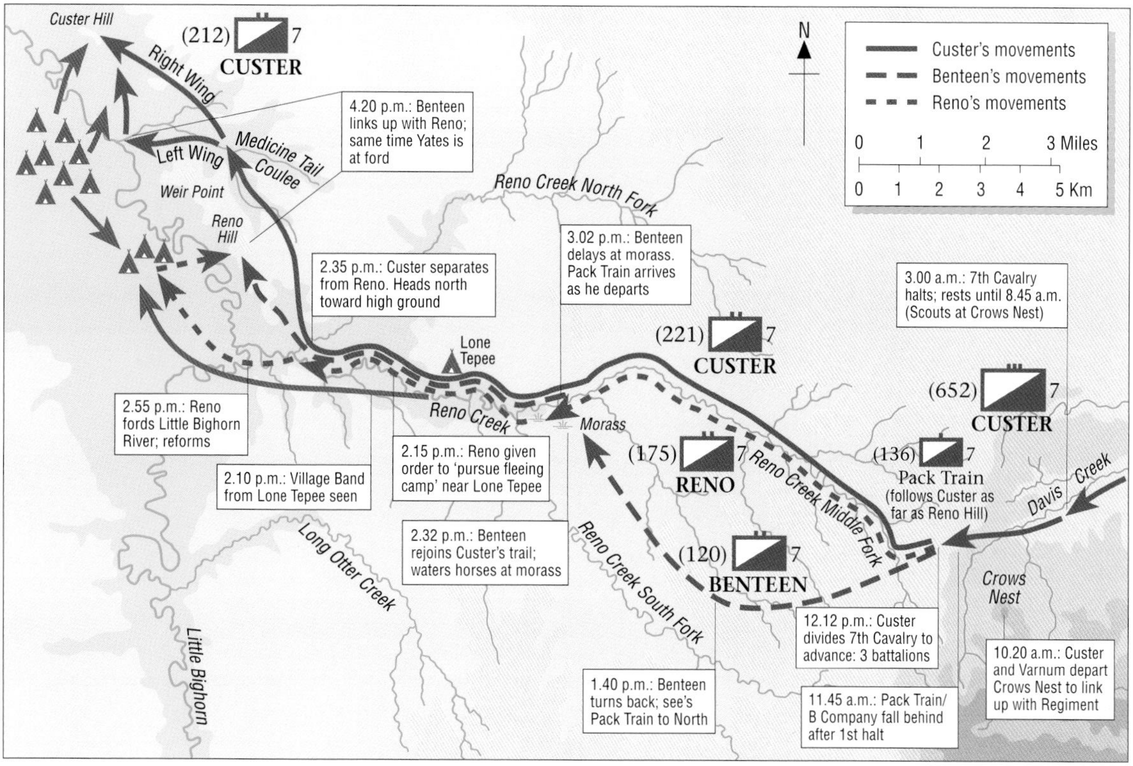

The regiment split as it passed the divide at 12.12 pm, Benteen wheeling to the left. Reno's battalion took the lead, descending what is now Reno Creek, on the left bank. Custer followed to the right and rear of Reno, to the right of the creek. For most of the day, all four groups were in sight of each other, and in supporting distance. During the approach, the pack train fell several miles behind, and Custer was forced by restrictive terrain to draw in close to Reno's right rear.

Several Indians were seen ahead of the column, causing a bit of excitement amongst the troopers. About 45 minutes into the scout, Benteen could see the main body a mile to his right. Lt. Godfrey recalled, 'During the march to the left, we could see occasionally the battalion under Custer, distinguished by the troop mounted on gray horses [E Company], marching at a rapid gait. Two or three times we heard loud cheering and also some few shots, but the occasion of these demonstrations is not known.'

The main body followed both sides of the creek and re-converged near a swampy morass at about 1.20 pm. They watered their horses and moved out again. By 1.40 pm Benteen, having seen nothing but empty valleys, turned back toward Custer. He could see the pack train following Custer's trail as he turned about. The advance was proceeding methodically as they approached the 'Lone Tepee' seen earlier from the Crow's Nest. Custer waved Reno's battalion over to the right bank of the creek just before 2.00 pm. As the two columns trotted beside each other they kicked up clouds of dust, visible for miles.

RENO ATTACKS

Some of the Indian scouts halted at the 'Lone Tepee'. This had been Sitting Bull's camp site on 16 June. A dead Sans Arc warrior, a casualty from the Rosebud Battle, lay inside the tepee. When Custer halted, Fred Girard, one of the civilian scouts, pointed and yelled out to him, 'Here are your Indians General, running like devils!' A few miles ahead Custer could see a fleeing village band of over 100 Indians. They were Cheyenne, moving to join the main camp, five miles ahead. To Custer, a main village was not yet discovered, but he immediately ordered a pursuit.

At about 2.15 pm Custer gave the following order to Reno. 'The Indians are about two miles and a half ahead. They are on the jump. Go forward as fast as you think proper, and charge them wherever you find them, and I will support you.' About 60 Cheyenne warriors were with the fleeing band. They turned and defiantly taunted the leading scouts, staying just ahead of the advance, as they withdrew toward the Little Big Horn.

With no report by then of any main camp, Custer would have been expecting numerous smaller camps, like the one he was now chasing. Each of his battalions were capable of flushing out anything they encountered like this. He instructed the Arikara scouts to go ahead and capture or drive off any Indian pony herd they found and deprive the enemy of their mobility. They hesitated, quite certain a large hostile camp was up ahead.

Meanwhile, Benteen was several miles to the rear, returning to Custer's trail at 2.30 pm. His troopers trotted to the morass, and watered their horses for 20 minutes. Benteen was criticised by his company commanders for delaying when shots were heard up ahead. Captain Wier impatiently departed with D Company, and the rest moved out at 3.03 pm, just as the pack train arrived. They walked on to the 'Lone Tepee'.

By 2.45 pm, as Reno's lead company approached the Little Big Horn River, the fleeing party had disappeared into the woods around the forks. Reno forded the river at about 2.55 pm, as Custer halted by the North Fork of Reno Creek to water his horses. Reno's troops also halted to water their horses . There was no sense of urgency yet. Custer decided to move north along the near side of the river. He rode away from his column, toward the high ground, to get a better view of the valley.

Sitting Bull had received reports of the soldiers' presence, but most of the Indians were still unaware of their proximity. Those warriors who had seen the 7th Cavalry approaching arrived just ahead of Reno. The appearance of the soldier's column threw the immense camp into turmoil. Custer had achieved a general surprise. As the non-combatants began their drill of breaking camp, the warriors went to meet the threat.

After Reno re-formed on the far side of the Little Big Horn River he saw a long flat plain stretching ahead for several miles. The band he was pursuing had passed ahead of him. Through the dust, three miles down the valley, he could see a portion of a larger village and much activity. Reno advanced two companies abreast, in line, and kept one following in reserve. The Indian scouts dashed off to the bench lands on the left flank, seeking to drive off the huge pony herd.

As they trotted forward, Reno's troopers caught glimpses of the

1st Lt. Edward S. Godfrey commanded Company K under Benteen. Godfrey had been with Custer since the Washita campaign of 1868, and during the 1877 Nez Percé campaign won the Medal of Honour. He retired a brigadier general, and protested the name of Major Reno on the Reno-Benteen battlefield monument. (Denver Public Library)

RIGHT *Custer's view west from the bluffs south of Wier Point. The full extent of the Indian village is obscured. Only the southern part of the camp would be visible from most positions south of Wier Point. (J. Thompson)*

Capt. Frederick W. Benteen, 1876, H Company commander, led a battalion of companies H, D and K on 25 June. Whenever Benteen was occupied, 1st Lt. Francis M. Gibson directed H Company. (Little Big Horn Battlefield National Monument)

grey-horse troop across the river on the bluffs. Some claimed to have seen Custer waving his hat. Custer, from his vantage point, could see more than Reno could, but only a portion of the village was visible. Custer expressed satisfaction that he had surprised the camp, and that they were fleeing. Shortly after 3.00 pm he dispatched Sergeant Daniel Kanipe, from C Company, with a message for Captain McDougal to bring the pack train forward. When near Captain Keogh he remarked, 'Keogh those Indians are running. If we can keep them at it we can afford to sacrifice half the horses in the command.' Several soldiers from Custer's battalion survived the battle because their horses gave out and they could not follow.

Reno ordered a charge, bringing all three companies into line. As he drew closer it became obvious that the camp was not in full flight. Dozens of warriors rode out to fight. Reno was about to charge into the southern end of an immense, two mile-long, hostile camp. He ordered a halt over 400 yards short. Trooper James Turley's horse bolted, carrying him into the midst of the camp. He was never found.

Reno had struck the south end of the camp where 260 lodges of the Hunkpapa Sioux were circled. This was Sitting Bull's tribe, and the heart of the resistance. Five other circles stretched along the river for up to two miles. (The camp is often credited as being twice as big as it was because it was moved that night to an adjacent spot.) The camp had over 1,000 lodges, which included circles of Miniconjou, Sans Arc, and a combined circle of Blackfoot, Brule and Two Kettle Sioux. At the northern end of the camp, which was the lead travelling position, were the Northern Cheyenne, followed by 240 lodges of Oglala Sioux. Warriors rushed from throughout the camp to meet Reno's attack.

The Hunkpapa warriors were the first to react. They fired at Reno's men from the edge of the village, screening the flight of the Indian non-combatants. Those who had ponies at hand rode them out to rescue the

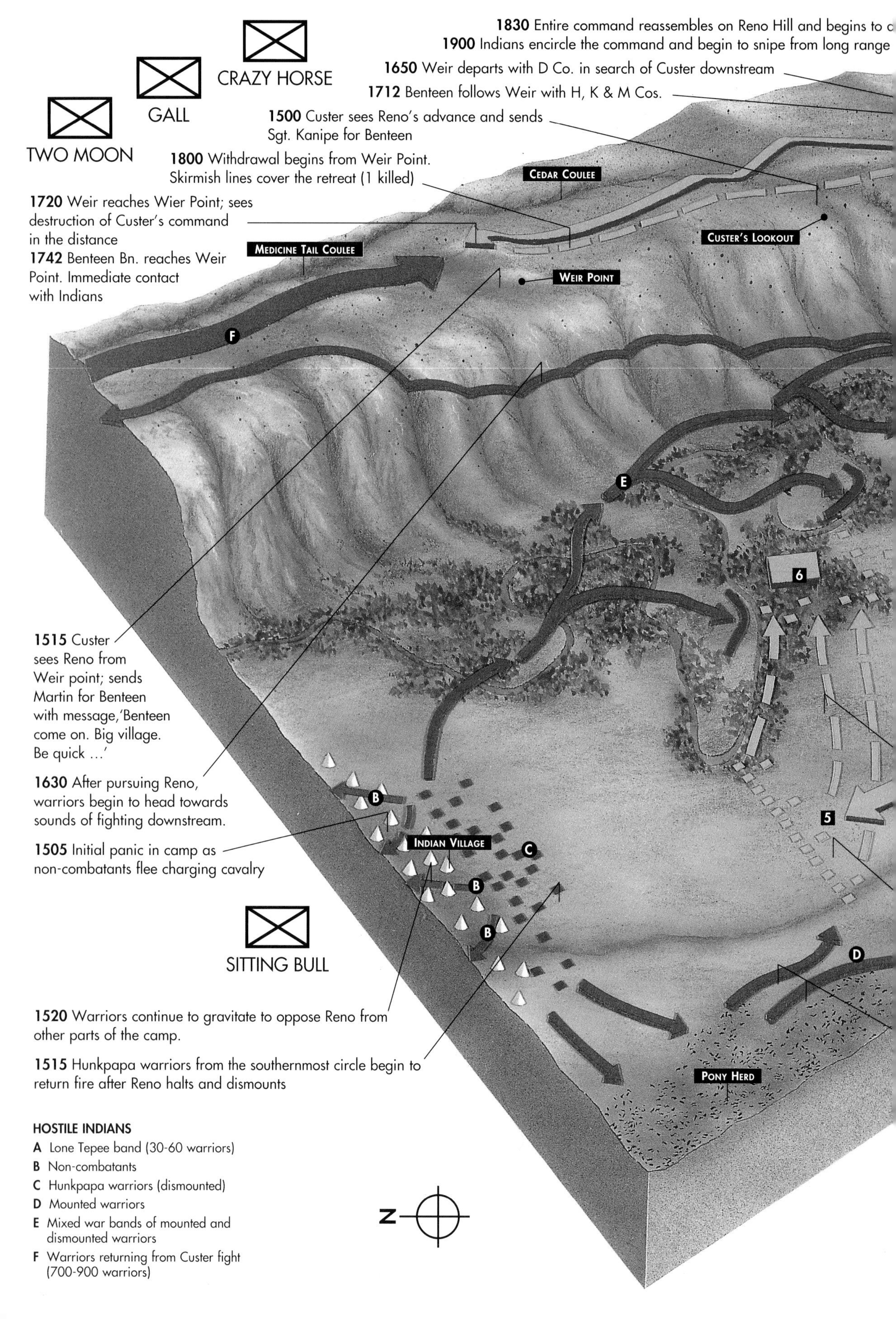

1830 Entire command reassembles on Reno Hill and begins to c
1900 Indians encircle the command and begin to snipe from long range
1650 Weir departs with D Co. in search of Custer downstream
1712 Benteen follows Weir with H, K & M Cos.
1500 Custer sees Reno's advance and sends Sgt. Kanipe for Benteen
1800 Withdrawal begins from Weir Point. Skirmish lines cover the retreat (1 killed)
1720 Weir reaches Wier Point; sees destruction of Custer's command in the distance
1742 Benteen Bn. reaches Weir Point. Immediate contact with Indians
CRAZY HORSE
GALL
TWO MOON
CEDAR COULEE
CUSTER'S LOOKOUT
MEDICINE TAIL COULEE
WEIR POINT
F
E
6
1515 Custer sees Reno from Weir point; sends Martin for Benteen with message,'Benteen come on. Big village. Be quick ...'
1630 After pursuing Reno, warriors begin to head towards sounds of fighting downstream.
1505 Initial panic in camp as non-combatants flee charging cavalry
B
INDIAN VILLAGE
C
B
B
5
D
SITTING BULL
1520 Warriors continue to gravitate to oppose Reno from other parts of the camp.
1515 Hunkpapa warriors from the southernmost circle begin to return fire after Reno halts and dismounts
PONY HERD
HOSTILE INDIANS
A Lone Tepee band (30-60 warriors)
B Non-combatants
C Hunkpapa warriors (dismounted)
D Mounted warriors
E Mixed war bands of mounted and dismounted warriors
F Warriors returning from Custer fight (700-900 warriors)
N

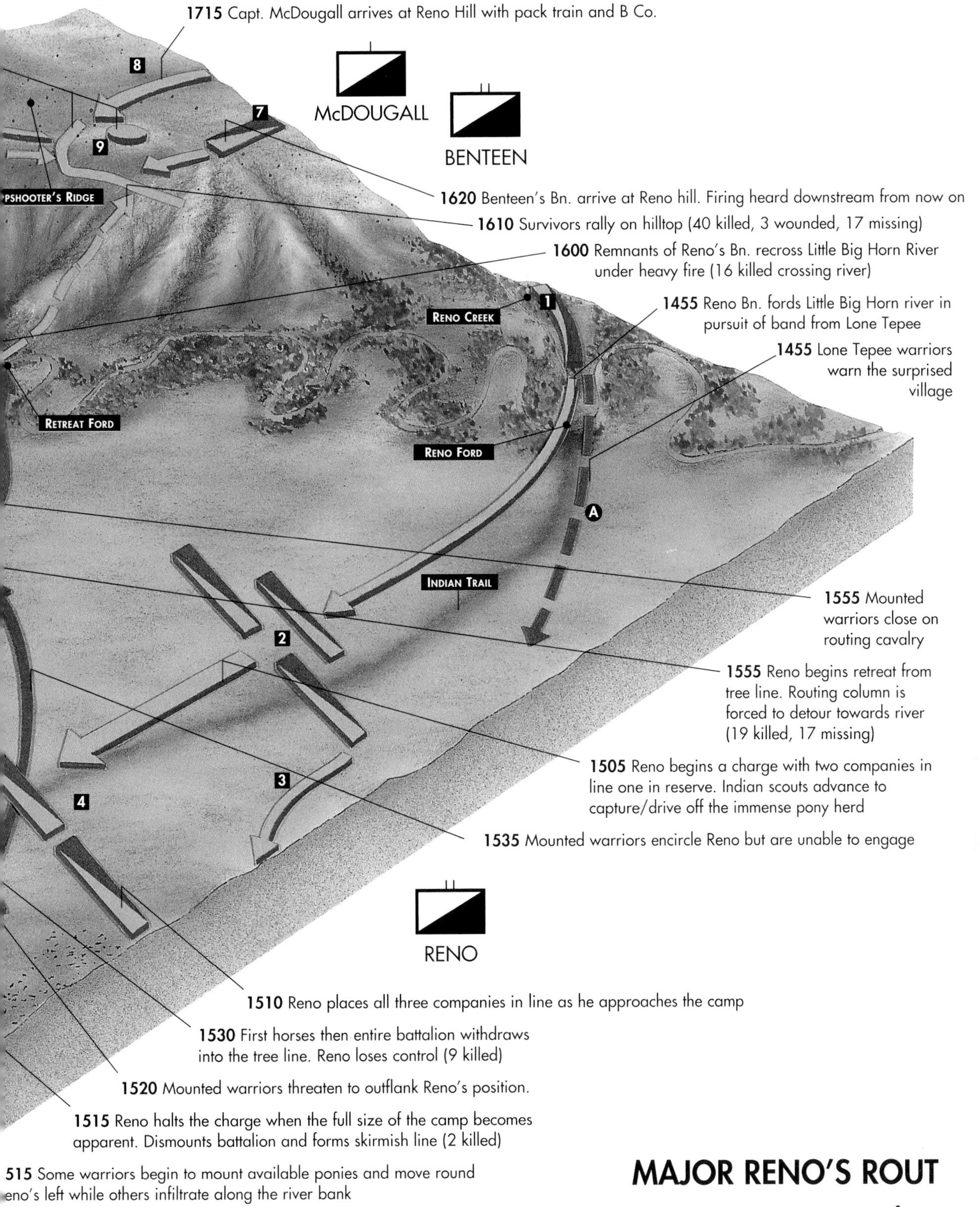
1715 Capt. McDougall arrives at Reno Hill with pack train and B Co.
McDOUGALL
BENTEEN
8
7
9
'PSHOOTER'S RIDGE
1620 Benteen's Bn. arrive at Reno hill. Firing heard downstream from now on
1610 Survivors rally on hilltop (40 killed, 3 wounded, 17 missing)
1600 Remnants of Reno's Bn. recross Little Big Horn River under heavy fire (16 killed crossing river)
RENO CREEK
1
1455 Reno Bn. fords Little Big Horn river in pursuit of band from Lone Tepee
1455 Lone Tepee warriors warn the surprised village
RETREAT FORD
RENO FORD
A
INDIAN TRAIL
1555 Mounted warriors close on routing cavalry
2
1555 Reno begins retreat from tree line. Routing column is forced to detour towards river (19 killed, 17 missing)
1505 Reno begins a charge with two companies in line one in reserve. Indian scouts advance to capture/drive off the immense pony herd
3
4
1535 Mounted warriors encircle Reno but are unable to engage
RENO
1510 Reno places all three companies in line as he approaches the camp
1530 First horses then entire battalion withdraws into the tree line. Reno loses control (9 killed)
1520 Mounted warriors threaten to outflank Reno's position.
1515 Reno halts the charge when the full size of the camp becomes apparent. Dismounts battalion and forms skirmish line (2 killed)
515 Some warriors begin to mount available ponies and move round
eno's left while others infiltrate along the river bank

7TH CAVALRY REGT.

1 Reno's Battalion
2 Reno's Bn.; two companies in line, one in reserve
3 Indian scouts
4 Reno's Bn.; all three companies in line
5 Reno's Bn.; dismounted skirmish line.
6 Reno's defensive position in copse of trees
7 Benteen's Battalion
8 Pack Train
9 Reno's survivors, Benteen's Bn., Pack train & escorts

MAJOR RENO'S ROUT

25 June 1876, 1455-1900, as seen from the west. Reno's initial advance and his subsequent retreat and rout to Reno Hill. The arrival of Benteen and the mule train helps to stabilise the situation

pony herd. The boys guarding the herds attempted to drive them toward the camp. Initially there were very few warriors to meet Reno, but their numbers surged as each grabbed his weapon and any available pony and went toward the shooting.

Reno's battalion dismounted, and every fourth man led horses to the rear. A skirmish line with less than 100 troopers fired toward the camp. Indian resistance increased as mounted warriors fanned out on Reno's left flank, a few circling to his rear. Several braves rode up and down in front of the skirmish line, daring the soldiers to shoot at them. Other Sioux leaders accumulated their personal followings and encouraged others to join them as they rode to the flanks and rear of the skirmish line. The cavalry men sent runners to get more carbine ammunition from their saddlebags.

The right flank of the skirmish line was secure on the riverbank, but to the left stretched wide open terrain. A detail from M Company cleared a copse of trees near the river bank, and the cavalry mounts were secured there. Reno had only lost one man at this point, but at 3.30 pm, fearing encirclement, he ordered a withdrawal. Private Theodore Goldin recounted: '... we were forced to face about and endeavour to repel their advances until we could get our horses into the timber, in which attempt several horses were shot, and two or three stampeded. Soon after this we retired into the timber, where we had better protection, and resumed the fight.'

Short Bull yelled to Crazy Horse as his following arrived, 'You are too late, you've missed the fight!' Crazy Horse held his warriors back from the engagement. The cavalry skirmishers shifted to the woods and established a hasty defence. When Reno withdrew, so did his scouts. The overwhelming size of the herd and the defending Sioux prevented the scouts from driving many of the ponies away. Those that had stolen a few fled with them back down the trail.

Above *View east from Reno's first skirmish line position south of the Indian camp. It is on the higher bluffs to the left (1.5 miles away) that Custer was spotted during Reno's initial charge.*

Above right *View east from Reno's first skirmish line position. It is about here that Reno halted his charge and dismounted to fire into the Indian camp. He subsequently ordered his battalion into the tree-line along the river. (J. Thompson)*

Short Bull was a Brule Sioux medicine man, and a 31-year-old protégé of Sitting Bull in 1876. In 1890 he and Kicking Bear were the principal leaders of the 'Ghost Dance' movement, which resulted in the infamous Wounded Knee incident, and Sitting Bull's death. (Little Big Horn Battlefield National Monument)

CUSTER SENDS FOR BENTEEN

'Benteen come on. Big village. Be quick. Bring packs. P.S. Bring packs.'

CUSTER'S LAST MESSAGE, 3.20 PM, 25 JUNE 1876

Custer moved his battalion north. The steep bluffs along the Little Big Horn concealed his movement from the valley. Lt. Cooke, Custer's adjutant, caught up to him with a message from Fred Girard that the Indians were not fleeing, but riding out to fight Reno. Custer, Cooke and a small escort rode to the bluffs near Wier Point. It was here that Custer got his first full view of the enormous camp and the mass of Indians in it. Thousands of non-combatants were fleeing to the north, while the warriors were moving to engage Reno. Reno had not yet withdrawn into the wood-line. Custer got his last view of Reno's battalion, skirmishing with the hostiles at the southern end of the village.

Custer returned to his column. He sent a second message at 3.20 pm via trumpeter John Martin, an Italian immigrant with limited language skills. Lt. Cooke scribbled a quick note for Benteen and handed it to Martin. It read, 'Benteen come on. Big village. Be quick. Bring packs. P.S. Bring packs.' Custer would need the additional troopers to continue any offensive actions. He was still in an offensive mode, and he cut north, paralleling the river and its steep, 100-foot banks.

This is the decisive point in the Battle of the Little Big Horn. Custer, having seen the size of the village, and Reno's engagement, decided to remain in an offensive posture and continue north. By 3.45 pm his battalion had reached the top of Medicine Tail Coulee, the first passable terrain leading toward the hostile village. A few scattered warriors were near the coulee, but evaded the first shots. The scouts Mitch Boyer and Crow Curley caught up to Custer at 4.00 pm and updated him on Reno's plight.

CAMPAIGN CLIMAX, 25 JUNE 1876

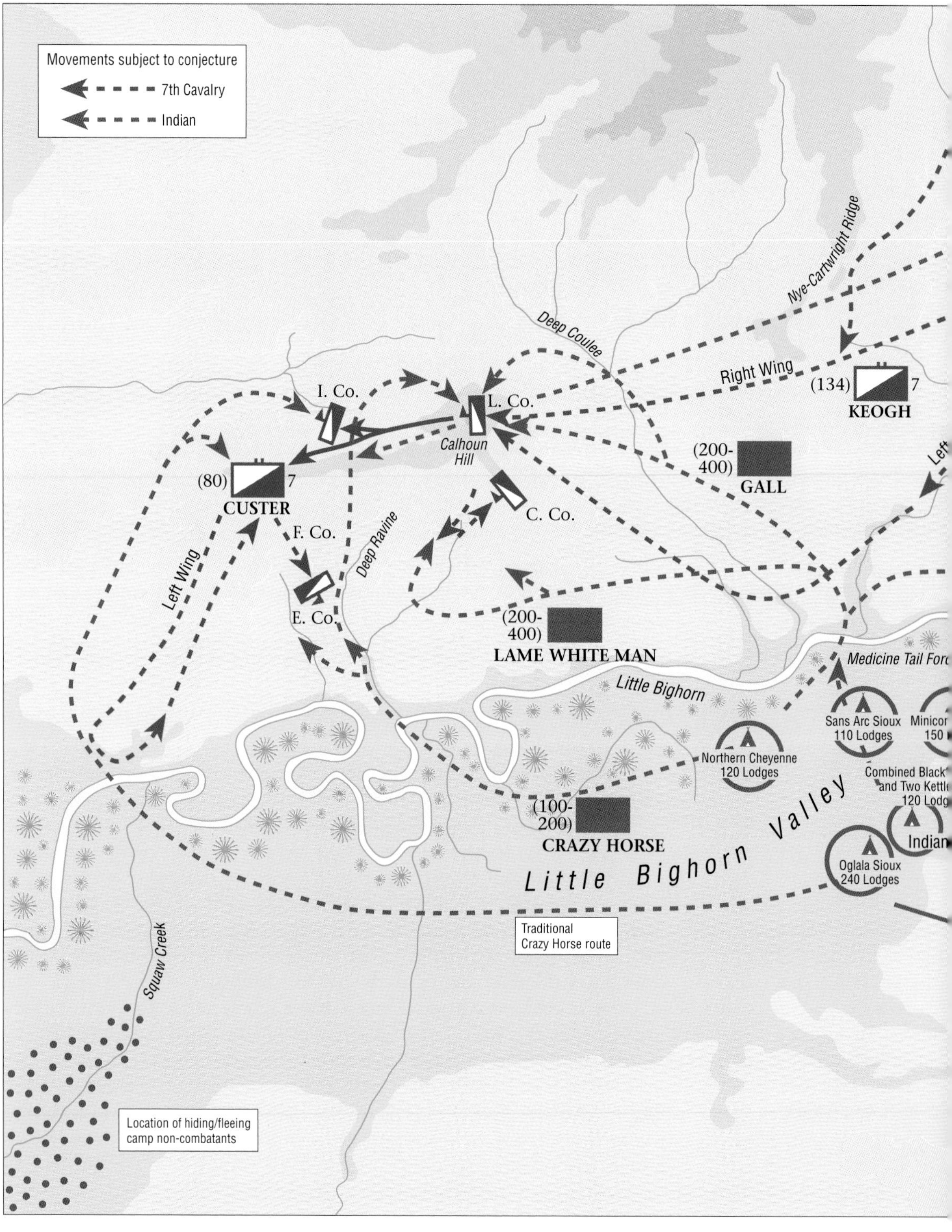

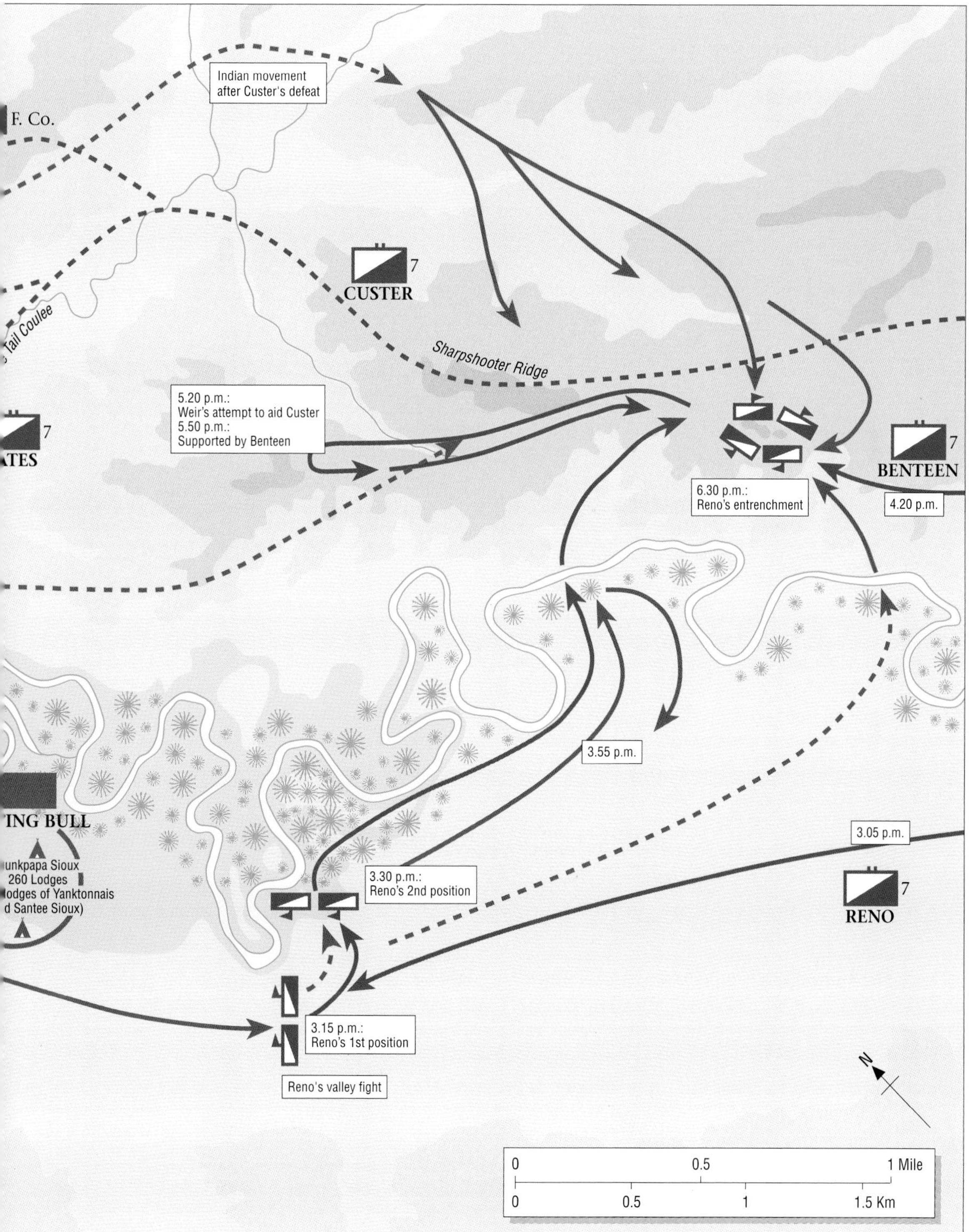

Indian movement after Custer's defeat
F. Co.
7
CUSTER
Tail Coulee
Sharpshooter Ridge
5.20 p.m.: Weir's attempt to aid Custer 5.50 p.m.: Supported by Benteen
7
TES
7
BENTEEN
6.30 p.m.: Reno's entrenchment
4.20 p.m.
3.55 p.m.
ING BULL
unkpapa Sioux 260 Lodges odges of Yanktonnais d Santee Sioux)
3.05 p.m.
3.30 p.m.: Reno's 2nd position
7
RENO
3.15 p.m.: Reno's 1st position
Reno's valley fight
N
0 0.5 1 Mile
0 0.5 1 1.5 Km

RENO PANICS

'Mount up ... Dismount ... Remount!' RENO, 3:55 PM

The riverbank formed a natural breastwork where Reno's battalion defended. The three companies formed a tight perimeter in the dense underbrush with the horses and additional ammo to their rear. Warriors swarmed about them but were kept at bay. Mounted warriors encircled Reno's position, some crossing the river to get around him. Others worked their way through the brush and trees, infiltrating along the river bank. In the confusion, Reno lost control of his subordinates. He had defended the position for something less than 20 minutes when he again, very suddenly, decided to withdraw.

Without ordering a bugle call, Major Reno mounted his horse and called for the battalion to 'mount up'. He instructed a few subordinates to assemble, in columns of fours, in a clearing. Many did not hear the orders. There was no security posted, and several warriors crept through the underbrush and fired a volley at close range. A trooper screamed as he was hit, and the Indian scout Bloody Knife was killed instantly as he mounted his pony next to Reno. Bloody Knife was shot in head, splattering blood and brains over Reno's uniform and face.

Major Reno was frightfully unnerved, and issued a series of contradicting orders to dismount and then mount up again. More confusion spread as the firefight continued. Some soldiers misunderstood the commands, while others were completely oblivious to Reno's location or intentions. Reno had lost his hat and tied a red bandanna around his head. Looking like a mad man, he bolted out of the wood line and shouted, 'Any of you men who wish to live, make your escape – follow me!'

View west from Wier Point into the Little Big Horn Valley. From here Custer would have had his first full view of the Indian camp, in full flight. Warriors were rushing to engage Reno to the south and the non-combatants were breaking camp or fleeing to the north. The river winds through the tree-line in the foreground.
(J. Thompson)

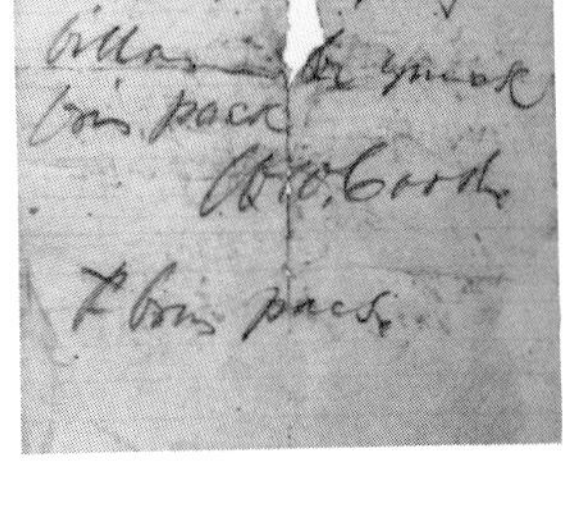
Benteen.
Come on. Big Village.
Be quick. Bring Packs.
P.S. Bring Packs.
W.W. Cooke

Fallen Foe *by Charles Schreyvogel. When Reno's battalion 'charged' out of the wood-line the Indians initially recoiled, evading the apparent shock attack. As soon as it was evident that the soldiers were fleeing in disorder, the hostiles surged forward again and overtook the column. (Little Big Horn Battlefield National Monument)*

RENO RETREATS

'When we came out of the woods there were a great many Indians scampering along with their rifles across the saddle, working their Winchesters on the column.' Lt. Varnum

The withdrawal quickly became a confused rout as the panicked troopers, Reno in the lead, fled back toward the river. He would later claim his flight back across the Little Big Horn River was a charge, but as civilian scout Fred Girard described it: 'The Indians picked off the troops at will ... It was a rout, not a charge!' When it was obvious the troopers were in full retreat, the mass of mounted warriors surged forward to exploit their vulnerability. The sheer numbers in their path caused the column to veer left toward the river's closest point.

Those who didn't initially get the word to escape quickly tried to follow; others hid in the timber. Many were isolated and cut down. The civilian scout 'Lonesome' Charley Reynolds was killed when his horse was shot as he tried to catch up with the column. Lt. McIntosh, the G Company commander, lost his horse in the woods, but was given one by a trooper. As he fled he was surrounded and killed by 20 Indians. The soldier who gave up his horse survived by hiding near the riverbank.

It was a classic example of the Plains Indians deadliest tactic, and compared to a buffalo hunt. The hostiles, on fresh horses, were able to catch Reno's retreating forces rapidly. As the column became strung out, troopers were clubbed or shot out of the saddle by warriors who rode close beside them. Civilian interpreter Isaiah Dorman, the only black man with the expedition, turned and shot an Indian in the heart at close range. Dorman was subsequently trapped under his wounded horse and killed. There was no rear guard to keep the pursuing enemy at a distance. Both

Left *Upon seeing the Indian village and Reno's valley engagement from Wier Point, Custer gave trumpeter John Martin a verbal message for Benteen to come with his battalion and to bring the pack train. Lt. Cooke pencilled this note to ensure Benteen's receipt. Martin (or Giovanni Martini, as was his real name) was an Italian immigrant and no doubt had limited language skills. (U. S. Military Academy)*

Capt. Moylan and Lt. Varnum attempted to halt some of their soldiers, but panic had set in. Every man was for himself as they splashed down the banks into the river.

It was 4.00 pm. Reno had spent one hour in the valley of the Little Big Horn. He lost most of his men during the five minute dash to the river. Many warriors closed in on the fleeing troopers, fiing point-blank, while others gathered at the bank to pick off soldiers struggling in the water. Reno's adjutant, Lt. Hodgeson, was wounded and fell into the river. He crossed, holding the stirrup of a fleeing trooper, but was shot dead on the far bank. One corporal from G Company killed an Indian and stopped to take his scalp, waving it from the far bank.

The exhausted troopers were barely able to climb or spur their horses up the steep, 100-foot bluffs on the east bank of the Little Big Horn. Several men, including the surgeon Dr. DeWolf climbed the wrong bluffs – those occupied by Indians – on the east side of the river, and were shot and scalped in plain view of the of the routing troopers. Some of the men grabbed their horse's tail to be pulled uphill; others turned on the far side to fire at the pursuing hostiles. Lt. Hare opened fire and let out a rebel yell: 'If we've got to die, let's die like men! I'm a fightin' son of a bitch from Texas!'

The remnants of Reno's battalion began to rally on a hilltop at about 4.10 pm as the Indian pursuit slacked off. Of his 175-man command (140 troopers and 35 scouts), Reno had lost 40 dead, including three officers, and 37 missing. Thirteen wounded made it to the hilltop and of the missing, 17 were left in the woods during the retreat, and linked up later. Reno's men could hear gunfire downstream. The hostile warriors halted their pursuit, and headed north to engage Custer. A few dozen tarried, sniping at the hilltop position. The Sioux and Cheyenne leaders succeeded in diverting most of their braves from this engagement to meet another threat downstream.

1st Lt. Donald McIntosh was the G Company commander in Reno's battalion. He was killed during Reno's retreat, reportedly unhorsed and surrounded by 20-30 Indians. (Little Big Horn Battlefield National Monument)

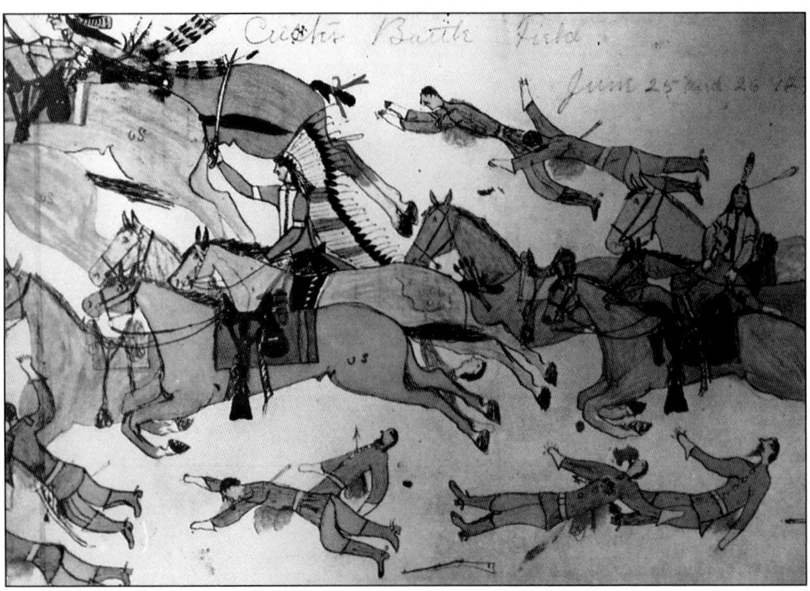

Left Native American artwork. The mounted warriors, on fresh ponies, were able to catch Reno's retreating soldiers easily. Troopers were shot or clubbed out of the saddle by warriors who rode beside them. (Amos Bad Heart Buffalo)

Capt. Miles Moylan commanded Company A, part of Reno's battalion. During Reno's retreat he attempted to form a rear guard but could not stop the panicked rout. (Little Big Horn Battlefield National Monument)

View from Reno Hill looking west. The Little Big Horn River is visible at the bottom of the ravine. Reno led his battalion in a panicked rout from the tree-line (top right) across the river without a rear guard. He left behind 40 dead and 37 missing; 13 wounded made it to the hilltop. (J. Thompson)

2nd Lt. Benjamin H. Hodgeson, Company B. During Reno's retreat he was knocked into the river and shot while holding the stirrup of a fleeing trooper. Reno spent 15 minutes searching for Hodgeson's body while the rest of his battalion re-organised on the hilltop. (Little Big Horn Battlefield National Monument)

BENTEEN ARRIVES

'We've had a big fight in the Valley, got whipped like hell, and I am damned glad to see you!' Lt. Luther Hare, 4.20 pm

Benteen had just passed the 'Lone Tepee' when he met Sergeant Kanipe, at about 3.38 pm. Kanipe had passed Custer's youngest brother Boston earlier, anxiously riding to join his brothers in the attack. By this time Reno's men were heavily engaged, and much gunfire could be heard up ahead. Benteen's men were eager to join the fight, and Kanipe yelled 'We've got them boys!' as he rode on to deliver his message to McDougal and the packs. His last impression had been that the Indians were surprised and fleeing. Kanipe met the pack train at 3.42 pm.

At 3.53 pm Benteen met Trumpeter Martin with Lt. Cooke's written message. Martin's horse was bleeding from a bullet wound, but he expressed to Benteen that the hostiles had 'skedaddled'. Benteen decided not to wait for the packs and rode on at a trot. Some Arikara scouts passed, making off with ponies they had captured in the valley. The scouts told Benteen 'heap Sioux', and pointed west. The sounds of gunfire intensified as he advanced, disputing with Weir over which trail to follow. Benteen hurried the pace and put his battalion into line as he neared the river. The warriors chasing Reno could see Benteen approach as they broke contact and moved back toward the village.

From a distance, Benteen saw Reno's routed troopers scrambling for the hilltop and rode toward them. He estimated there were over 1,000 Indians

Bunkie *by Charles Schreyvogel. During Reno's retreat there are several accounts of soldiers carrying their wounded or dismounted comrades to safety. Better trained Cavalry units, such as Custer's, practised such moves, but it took a skilled (and brave) horseman to execute something like this in the heat of a running battle. (Little Big Horn Battlefield National Monument)*

Sgt. Daniel Kanipe, a member of C Company, carried Custer's (verbal) order for McDougal to bring the pack train forward. As he rode back down the trail he passed Boston Custer, hurrying to his death. He informed Benteen and McDougal that the hostiles were fleeing. (Little Big Horn Battlefield National Monument)

in the valley, headed the other way. Reno met Benteen and exclaimed, 'For God's sake, Benteen, halt your command and help me! I've lost half my men!' Reno was still in shock, and turned and discharged his pistol towards the Indians, 900 yards away. Reno immediately led a detail back down the bluffs to search for his adjutant, Lt. Hodgeson. Reno had not reorganised his people into a defence, so Capt. Weir's company formed a dismounted skirmish line and engaged the few hostiles still firing at them. Benteen had his men redistribute their additional ammunition amongst Reno's demoralised men. Reno returned from his search when fired upon by the Indians, and at 4.40 pm sent Lt. Hare to find the pack train and bring the ammunition mules forward.

ADVANCE TO WIER POINT

Although continuous firing was heard downstream, Benteen and Reno decided to wait for the packs before seeking Custer. Many of the men heard distinct volleys, and speculated that it was a signal. Capt. Wier, who had seen Custer's message, moved his company toward the sound of the guns at about 4.50 pm. The ammunition mules arrived 20 minutes later, but only one 1,000 round case was opened. Benteen followed Wier at 5.12 pm with companies H, K and M. Capt. Wier and D Company reached the high point, (which now bears his name) at 5.20 pm. Benteen was not far behind, and Reno was also moving, with three companies, the pack train and the wounded.

From Wier Point the officers searched the horizon for signs of Custer. They could clearly see the village in the valley to their left, but the rolling hills to the north were obscured by gun smoke, dust clouds, and the afternoon glare. Initially, Wier saw one of Custer's swallow-tailed guidons fluttering above some distant horsemen, but closer inspection revealed it to be a band of Indians (no doubt counting coups with a captured guidon).

Capt. Thomas B. Wier, an experienced but often impetuous leader, commanded D Company. Extremely loyal to Custer, he held much contempt for Reno and distrust for Benteen. Denied permission to move his company to Custer's aid, he reportedly rode off by himself. This prompted his executive officer, 2nd Lt. Winfield S. Edgerly, to follow with D Company. Benteen and Reno eventually followed in support. (BYU Camp Collection)

View from Wier Point to Custer Hill, 3 miles north-west. The group of trees (centre) is the cemetery adjacent to Custer Hill. Wier's company halted here and through much dust saw 'a good many Indians galloping up and down and firing at objects on the ground'. (J. Thompson)

Lt. Edgerly, recalled, 'We saw a good many Indians galloping up and down and firing at objects on the ground.' Years later he admitted, 'We could see the bodies of Custer's men and horses with swarms of Indians.' These were the final moments of Custer's last stand.

When the shooting subsided, the victorious warriors began to converge on Wier Point. The four companies skirmished for a short while, but the position was untenable. At 6.00 pm Benteen ordered a withdrawal to Reno Hill. Company K formed a rear guard, and the remnants of the 7th Cavalry Regiment reassembled to defend the hilltop at 6.30 pm. The Indians were close on their heels and surrounded the position.

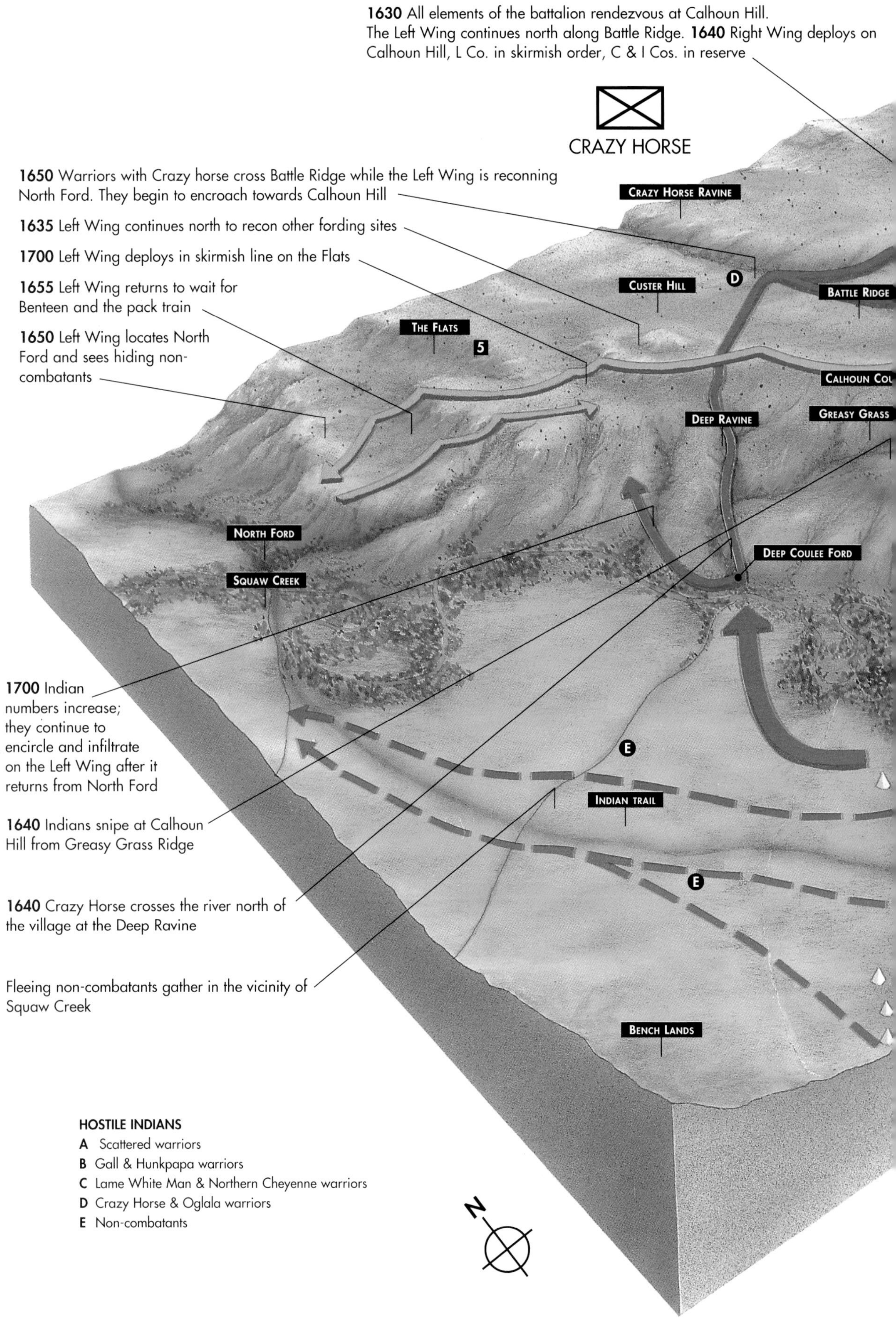
1630 All elements of the battalion rendezvous at Calhoun Hill. The Left Wing continues north along Battle Ridge. **1640** Right Wing deploys on Calhoun Hill, L Co. in skirmish order, C & I Cos. in reserve
CRAZY HORSE
1650 Warriors with Crazy horse cross Battle Ridge while the Left Wing is reconning North Ford. They begin to encroach towards Calhoun Hill
1635 Left Wing continues north to recon other fording sites
1700 Left Wing deploys in skirmish line on the Flats
1655 Left Wing returns to wait for Benteen and the pack train
1650 Left Wing locates North Ford and sees hiding non-combatants
Crazy Horse Ravine
Custer Hill
D
Battle Ridge
The Flats
5
Calhoun Cou
Deep Ravine
Greasy Grass
North Ford
Squaw Creek
Deep Coulee Ford
1700 Indian numbers increase; they continue to encircle and infiltrate on the Left Wing after it returns from North Ford
E
Indian trail
1640 Indians snipe at Calhoun Hill from Greasy Grass Ridge
E
1640 Crazy Horse crosses the river north of the village at the Deep Ravine
Fleeing non-combatants gather in the vicinity of Squaw Creek
Bench Lands
HOSTILE INDIANS
A Scattered warriors
B Gall & Hunkpapa warriors
C Lame White Man & Northern Cheyenne warriors
D Crazy Horse & Oglala warriors
E Non-combatants
N

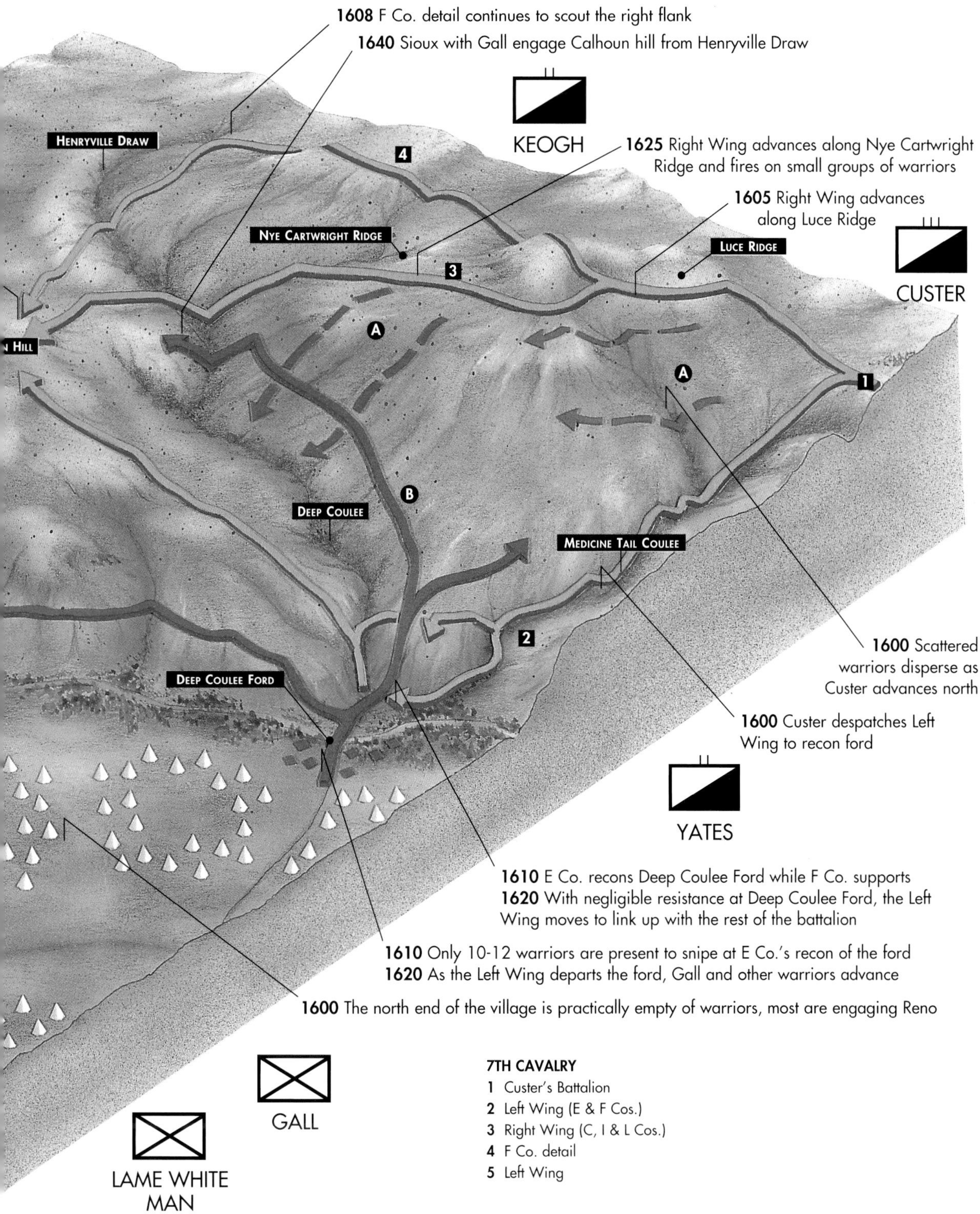

1608 F Co. detail continues to scout the right flank
1640 Sioux with Gall engage Calhoun hill from Henryville Draw
KEOGH
HENRYVILLE DRAW
4
1625 Right Wing advances along Nye Cartwright Ridge and fires on small groups of warriors
1605 Right Wing advances along Luce Ridge
NYE CARTWRIGHT RIDGE
LUCE RIDGE
CUSTER
3
A
N HILL
A
1
B
DEEP COULEE
MEDICINE TAIL COULEE
2
1600 Scattered warriors disperse as Custer advances north
DEEP COULEE FORD
1600 Custer despatches Left Wing to recon ford
YATES
1610 E Co. recons Deep Coulee Ford while F Co. supports
1620 With negligible resistance at Deep Coulee Ford, the Left Wing moves to link up with the rest of the battalion
1610 Only 10-12 warriors are present to snipe at E Co.'s recon of the ford
1620 As the Left Wing departs the ford, Gall and other warriors advance
1600 The north end of the village is practically empty of warriors, most are engaging Reno
GALL
LAME WHITE MAN
7TH CAVALRY
1 Custer's Battalion
2 Left Wing (E & F Cos.)
3 Right Wing (C, I & L Cos.)
4 F Co. detail
5 Left Wing

CUSTER'S ADVANCE

25 June 1876, 1600-1700, as seen from the south west. Custer's advance towards the north end of the village, the Left Wing's reconnaissance of Deep Coulee ford and the concentration on Battle Ridge

CUSTER'S LAST STAND

Captain George W. Yates, F Company commander and Custer's left wing commander. Yates had served with Custer since the Civil War. Custer had personally requested him for a staff position. Yates and up to 20 troopers from F Company were found dead near Custer. (Brigham Young University Camp Collection)

Traditional accounts of Custer's demise have him 'encountering an overwhelming number of hostiles at the centre of the village, his soldiers desperately fighting their way uphill, racing on their tired horses for a defensible hilltop, pursued by thousands of hostiles who all jumped on their horses and immediately counter attacked'. Crazy Horse is credited with 'leading another large body of warriors on a fast flanking ride up the west bank of the river, crossing two miles north, and sweeping in above Custer, catching him before he could consolidate on the summit. In less than 30 minutes, the entire element was surrounded. Eventually Custer and his immediate command was annihilated, fighting to the last man and the last cartridge, at the Little Big Horn'.[1]

It is a sensational and fatalist account, fostered mostly by Elizabeth Custer and those who sought to cover mistakes or further glorify the disaster as inevitable fate. The 'fatalist theories' are untrue, unfounded, and readily disproved by even cursory academic and archaeological research.

One of the most compelling and recent works to date is that of Dr. Richard A. Fox's *Archaeology, History, and Custer's Last Battle*. The following account is drawn from that archaeological template.

DESCENDING THE MEDICINE TAIL COULEE

'No one should charge yet, the soldiers are too many!'

MAD WOLF, CHEYENNE WARRIOR AT MEDICINE TAIL FORD.

The Custer battalion entered the Medicine Tail Coulee at about 3.45 pm, while Reno was still engaged in the valley. There were a few mounted warriors scurrying about the east side of the river, but they kept their distance. The half-breed scout Mitch Boyer and young Crow scout Curley had witnessed Reno's defeat, and informed Custer at 4.00 pm. Custer released the two scouts, but Boyer chose to stay. Curley departed to the east and watched Custer's defeat from over a mile away, disguised in a dead Sioux warrior's blanket.

Custer sent Captain Yates and the left wing (about 80 troopers) down

1 Author's account from a previous publication.

the Medicine Tail Coulee toward the village, either to conduct a reconnaissance or possibly also to draw the pressure off Reno's beleaguered battalion. The Medicine Tail Ford was located near the northern end of the village, where less than a dozen warriors opposed E Company at about 4.10

As part of Custer's command approached the river near the northern end of the village they encountered a growing number of hostiles. Gall had diverted hundreds of warriors from the Reno fight to meet Custer in the north. (Little Big Horn Battlefield National Monument)

The booklet cover for a Cyclorama of Custer's Last Stand. Printed in 1889, it shows the typical sensationalisation of the Little Big Horn battle. Much of the misconceived history of the battle is still reported today. (US National Archives)

1st Lt. Algernon E. Smith was the E Company, 'Grey Horse Troop' commander. His was the only E Company body found on Custer hill. The others were found spread along the line leading to and into Deep Ravine. (Little Big Horn Battlefield National Monument)

pm. A detachment approached the ford, while skirmishers fired across the river. One or more soldiers were shot at the water, possibly checking the river's fordability. Company F stood on the high ground 500 yards behind them in support. They fired a few volleys toward the village.

The battle had been raging for over an hour, and this end of the village was mostly empty. The non-combatants had fled, and most of the fighting men were either engaging Reno, escorting the non-combatants away or seeking ponies from the herd. About a dozen Indians, with the Sioux warrior White Cow Bull, returned fire at the soldiers, but neither side attempted to cross. The Oglala Sioux He Dog went west with others to 'get ready'. He arrived at the ford and helped shoot 'a few shots' across the river –'Not much shooting there.'

The number of warriors gradually increased. They didn't cross the ford until the troopers had started to leave. Smith and Yates employed skirmishers, in good order, to cover their movement up Deep Coulee toward Calhoun Hill. Warriors began to spill across the ford and ascend both the Medicine Tail and Deep coulees. It was now some 30 minutes after the Reno fight, and Gall had diverted hundreds of Hunkpapa, Sans Arc and Miniconjou warriors from the southern end of the camp to meet this new threat.

The Sioux, following Gall, shifted to the south of Calhoun Hill, while the Cheyenne following Two Moon and Lame White Man, massed behind the Greasy Grass Ridge. They crossed and fanned out to the coulees and ravines to the left and right, keeping their distance from Yates' skirmish lines. The Sioux encirclement tactics had begun.

While Smith and Yates were lightly engaged at the Medicine Tail Ford, the right wing deployed along Luce Ridge. A small detail of F Company troopers patrolled the eastern ridge-line as flank security. Scattered warriors skirmished with the right wing along Luce and Nye-Cartwright Ridge, but fled as the column advanced north. Both the left and right wings briefly linked up on Calhoun Hill at 4.30 pm. The Custer battalion was still in the offensive posture, able to move about the battlefield at will, brush-

Boston Custer was the youngest of the three brothers. He was signed on as a civilian guide, and accompanied the pack train. As the battle began he left the pack train to join his brothers. His arrival gave Custer critical information: that both Ryan's and Martin's messages had reached Reno, that Reno was en route, and that no Indians blocked the trail. (Little Big Horn Battlefield National Monument)

Indian squaws rush to break camp in the direction of Squaw Creek as Custer's troops rush into the settlement on the afternoon of 26 June 1876. This famous painting by Frederic Remington hangs in the Museum of Fine Art in Houston, Texas.

ing aside the light resistance wherever they deployed. The Indians continued to evade, harass and gather thier numbers.

Custer's youngest brother, Boston, had arrived by this time. As the shooting began he left the pack train to join his brothers. His arrival provided critical information that would affect Custer's decisions. Sergeant Ryan and Trumpeter Martin (with messages) had reached Reno and McDougal. Reno was en route, possibly close behind Boston, and the route was open – no Indians blocked the trail.

THE FLEEING VILLAGE

'[Custer] ... expected to find the squaws and children fleeing to the bluffs on the north, for in no other way do I account for his wide detour to the right .'

Lt. Godfrey

Two Moon, a prominent Northern Cheyenne war chief, led a band of warriors to infiltrate Custer's flank while Gall attacked from the south-west. The Cheyenne warriors were especially vindictive toward the white soldiers, their hatred inspired by the Washita massacre. (Little Big Horn Battlefield National Monument)

Custer's mission was to force the warriors to return to the reservation. His most effective method of achieving this was to destroy their homes and property, or capture the non-combatants and hold them hostage. After the skirmish at the ford, the mass of Indian women and children had fled north of the village and congregated in a series of streams and bluffs called Squaw Creek.

The non-combatants were the primary targets. Lt. Godfrey understood Custer's expected strategy as: ' ... attack on the families and the capture of the pony herds were in that event counted upon to strike consternation into the hearts of the warriors, and were elements for success'. According to Trumpeter Martin, Custer had expressed this intention to his subordinates before descending the Medicine Tail Coulee. With Benteen and the pack train present, he would have sufficient numbers to capture them.

Immediately after the two Custer battalion wings converged on Calhoun Hill, the left wing moved north along battle ridge to investigate any northern ford, and confirm the location of the non-combatants. The right wing sounded their trumpets and smartly executed the standard battle drill: Calhoun's L Company deployed to with skirmish, companies C and I in reserve. They began firing on the hostiles from the hill. Warriors attempting to interfere with Yates movement were suppressed, and Yates' troopers eventually moved, with little resistance, north-west along the Cemetery Ridge.

Custer and his staff probably accompanied Yates' wing in this reconnaissance. They rode about a mile beyond Custer Hill, within sight of the north ford and Squaw Creek. Across the river, thousands of Indian non-combatants were seeking refuge. Custer would need the additional 300 men from Benteen and the pack train before he could do more. Correspondent Mark Kellogg was killed near the river, where shots were exchanged with a few Cheyenne. The left wing then retraced its steps, moving along the flats, back toward Cemetery Ridge.

After the Reno fight, Crazy Horse spent up to 20 minutes conducting a spiritual ritual, and sprinkling dust from a prairie dog mound over himself. The warriors with him grew impatient, but when they galloped through to the north end of the camp, more warriors flocked to follow his band. While Custer and the left wing were beyond Cemetery Ridge, Crazy Horse and his mounted following crossed the Little Big Horn River at the mouth of the Deep Ravine, just north of the village. They ascended through the Deep ravine and crossed the mile-long Battle Ridge far to the north of the right wing, then took covered positions in the ravines along the east side of the ridge and began to infiltrate towards the right wing. With Gall approaching Calhoun Hill from the south, the Cheyenne leader, Lame White Man, to the west, and Crazy Horse now to the east, the encirclement was complete.

It was about this time, 4.50 pm, that Capt. Weir departed Reno Hill with D Company. Custer's left wing returned to Cemetery Ridge and deployed in skirmish formation, with E Company taking up a position near Custer Hill and F Company just below it. Indian aggressiveness intensified as their numbers rapidly increased. They began to close in from all directions. Cheyenne war chief Two Moons and Runs the Enemy attempted to stampede the grey horses (E Company) near Cemetery Ridge, but were deterred by carbine fire. The Custer battalion waited, looking south-east for Benteen. Calhoun and Keogh were on Calhoun Hill, Custer, Yates and

1st Lt. James Calhoun, Company L commander, was Custer's brother-in-law. Calhoun's company was dismounted in skirmish lines when overwhelmed and destroyed on the hill that now bears his name. Very few escaped to Custer's position three-quarters of a mile away. (Denver Public Library)

This detail from Theodore B. Pitman's painting would more accurately portray Calhoun's company as it collapsed and was engulfed from all sides by Sioux and Cheyenne warriors. Portions of the lines stood and grouped together, while others fled. Few escaped. (Little Big Horn Battlefield National Monument)

Smith on Cemetery Ridge. The skirmishing continued for 20 or more minutes, as the hostiles continued to infiltrate.

CALHOUN HILL COLLAPSE

Captain Keogh, Custer's right wing commander, had deployed the three companies on Calhoun Hill in the standard US Cavalry textbook formation. Calhoun's L Company formed a semicircle skirmish line on the forward (south-western) slopes of Calhoun Hill, their horse holders beyond the crest. C and I companies were deployed in reserve on the reverse slope. At first L Company skirmishers kept the accumulating warriors at bay. Some dashed about on horseback, daring to ride close to the soldiers, while others crept in as close as they could.

As warriors continued to arrive from the Reno fight, L Company became more heavily engaged from the west and south. The horses were in jeopardy, and their holders were taking fire from Calhoun Coulee. Keogh dispatched C Company, led by Lt. Harington, to charge west into Calhoun Coulee and dislodge a small group of warriors who were threatening the horses and men. The charge failed because the troopers were exposed to intense fire when they came into range of Greasy Grass Ridge and other positions. The survivors fled back to Calhoun Hill and were immediately pursued by mounted warriors led by Cheyenne chief Lame White Man. Company L, under Lt. Calhoun, shifted their skirmish line to the right to cover C Company's retreat.

Warriors to the south, following Gall, seized the opportunity. They rushed up the southern approaches to Calhoun Hill in an intense blaze of rifle fire. This sudden shock triggered a collapse of the position, since a few troopers panicked and attempted to flee, encouraging many more warriors to surge forward. They charged in, mounted and on foot, from several directions, engaging in ferocious hand-to-hand combat. This is where the fighting was the most intense, and the Indian received most casualties, including Lame White Man. Yellow Nose, a Cheyenne warrior, dashed forward and snatched the L Company guidon. (This may have been witnessed

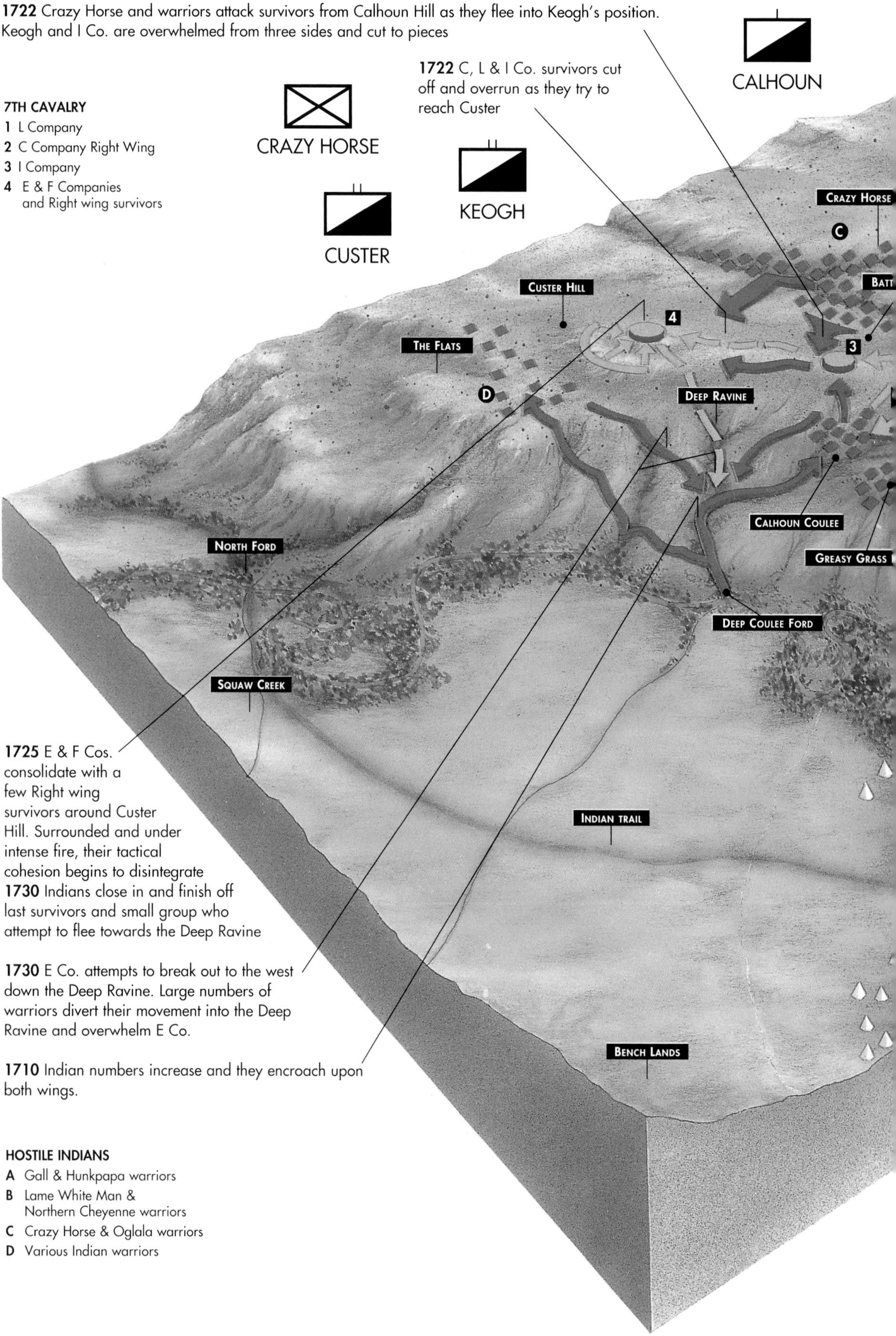

1722 Crazy Horse and warriors attack survivors from Calhoun Hill as they flee into Keogh's position. Keogh and I Co. are overwhelmed from three sides and cut to pieces
1722 C, L & I Co. survivors cut off and overrun as they try to reach Custer
CALHOUN
7TH CAVALRY
1 L Company
2 C Company Right Wing
3 I Company
4 E & F Companies and Right wing survivors
CRAZY HORSE
KEOGH
CUSTER
CRAZY HORSE
C
BATT
CUSTER HILL
4
THE FLATS
3
D
DEEP RAVINE
CALHOUN COULEE
GREASY GRASS
NORTH FORD
DEEP COULEE FORD
SQUAW CREEK
1725 E & F Cos. consolidate with a few Right wing survivors around Custer Hill. Surrounded and under intense fire, their tactical cohesion begins to disintegrate
1730 Indians close in and finish off last survivors and small group who attempt to flee towards the Deep Ravine
INDIAN TRAIL
1730 E Co. attempts to break out to the west down the Deep Ravine. Large numbers of warriors divert their movement into the Deep Ravine and overwhelm E Co.
BENCH LANDS
1710 Indian numbers increase and they encroach upon both wings.
HOSTILE INDIANS
A Gall & Hunkpapa warriors
B Lame White Man & Northern Cheyenne warriors
C Crazy Horse & Oglala warriors
D Various Indian warriors

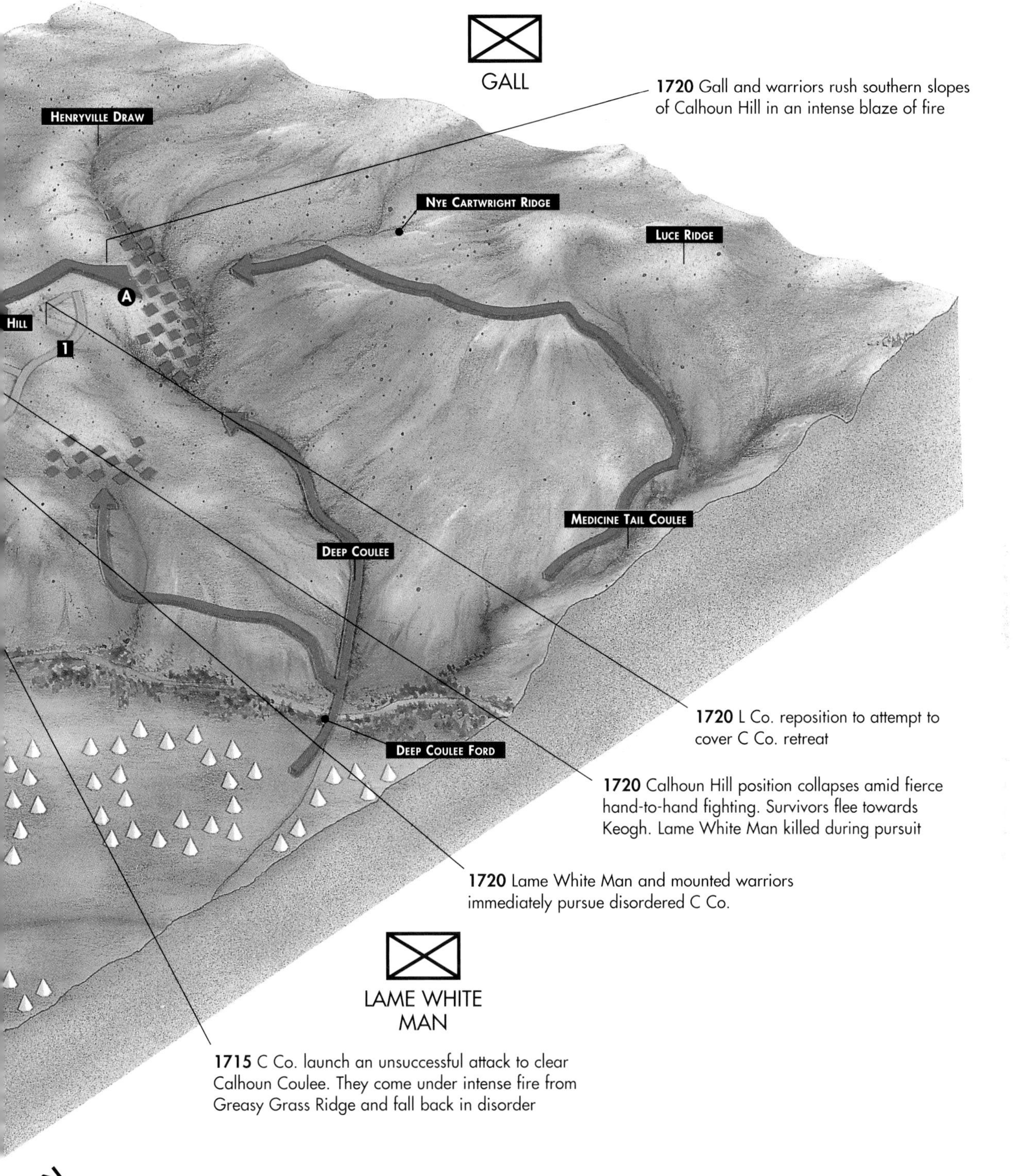
GALL
1720 Gall and warriors rush southern slopes of Calhoun Hill in an intense blaze of fire
Henryville Draw
Nye Cartwright Ridge
Luce Ridge
A
Hill
1
Medicine Tail Coulee
Deep Coulee
1720 L Co. reposition to attempt to cover C Co. retreat
Deep Coulee Ford
1720 Calhoun Hill position collapses amid fierce hand-to-hand fighting. Survivors flee towards Keogh. Lame White Man killed during pursuit
1720 Lame White Man and mounted warriors immediately pursue disordered C Co.
LAME WHITE MAN
1715 C Co. launch an unsuccessful attack to clear Calhoun Coulee. They come under intense fire from Greasy Grass Ridge and fall back in disorder
N

THE COLLAPSE OF CUSTER'S COMMAND

25 June 1876, 1700-1730, as seen from the south west.
Calhoun's position is overrun and Keogh's position collapses in the pursuit. The Indians close in on Custer and overwhelm him with firepower and numbers

by Captain Wier two miles away, but it is more likely he saw the guidon being carried about as a coup-stick later in the fight.)

Some soldiers were cut down fleeing, others grouped together and made easy targets for the warriors with bows. Lt. Calhoun was killed in one of these small groups. Some of the soldiers on horseback fled the 600 yards toward Keogh's position, but most of those on foot were ridden down.

KEOGH'S POSITION IS OVERRUN

'Another [Indian] charge was made and they retreated along the line of the ridge. It looked like a stampede of buffalo.' RUNS THE ENEMY

As Calhoun's company collapsed, engulfed by Sioux and Cheyenne Warriors, Keogh's I Company deployed to engage the pursuing warriors. They were unable to react fast enough, and were shaken by the sudden turn of events. When the survivors fled towards I Company, tactical cohesion disintegrated there also. Crazy Horse and his following were

Captain Miles W. Keogh, an experienced Indian fighter, commanded Company L. He was Custer's right wing commander, and deployed the three companies on Calhoun Hill in the standard US Cavalry textbook formation. Capt. Keogh was killed with a small group of his soldiers on the eastern slope of the ridge. Crazy Horse led a group of warriors who swept in on Keogh from the east just as the other warriors pursued C and L companies from the south and west. (Little Big Horn Battlefield National Monument)

Left Red Horse, the Miniconjou war chief who fought both Reno and Custer. He was involved in hand to hand fighting during the overrunning and pursuit of Keogh's company, and claimed to have picked up several cartridge belts still full of ammunition. He made several dozen drawings depicting the battle. (Little Big Horn Battlefield National Monument)

This spectacular painting by William R Leigh focuses on the Indians riding around the besieged troopers (in typical Hollywood fashion). This perception is possible since there are accounts of mounted groups of warriors dashing about the battlefield; however the ratio of casualties shown here is unlikely. Mounted, moving hostiles were impossible to hit from any distance.

Rain in the Face, an experienced and renowned Hunkpapa war chief who was a leader in the Fetterman battle and the Red Cloud wars. He was captured, but escaped from the Fort Lincoln Stockade. After the Little Big Horn battle he boasted to have cut out and eaten the heart of Tom Custer as an act of revenge for his imprisonment. Numerous accounts contradict this claim. (Little Big Horn Battlefield National Monument)

encroaching from the ravine north-east of Keogh, in perfect position to attack. They swept in on all three companies from the east, as the other warriors pursued C and L companies from the south and west. The entire element was surrounded and cut to pieces.

The left wing was also under some pressure as the hostiles closed in. Pinned, and out of supporting fire range, Custer must have watched in horror as events rapidly unfolded before him, less than a mile down the ridge. There was little opportunity to react, for within a matter of minutes the right wing had disintegrated.

Absolute chaos reigned as more frenzied warriors surged forward and terrified troopers tried to flee. More soldiers bunched together and resisted before being killed or forced to run away. Captain Keogh was killed with a small group of his men on the eastern slope of the ridge. The fight moved along the ridge from Calhoun Hill to Custer Hill. Many of the soldiers were dismounted, and more dead horses were found in this area than anywhere else on the battlefield. Only a handful of troopers managed to break through to the temporary safety of the left wing. Three company guidons were now being carried about the battlefield as coup-sticks. The dead were quickly stripped of their weapons and trophies, and the wounded were dispatched, while the shocked survivors on Custer Hill looked on. Over half the battalion was gone; the remainder were surrounded and outnumbered.

ESCAPE ATTEMPTS

'15 or 20 soldiers ... jumped up and started to run towards the river down the [Deep] ravine. [They] did not fire back and mounted Indians killed them.' Big Beaver

The left wing was able to maintain tactical cohesion as they deployed to receive about 20 left wing fugitives. A skirmish line from E Company opened fire on the pursuing Indians, checking the warriors' advance along

Custer's Last Battle by Elk Eber. This detail, showing a heroic struggle to the death on Custer Hill, is typical of the so-called 'fatalist theory' accounts of Custer's demise. Archaeological evidence and Indian accounts disprove this theory. It is doubtful that any of Custer's group were left standing as warriors closed in to finish them off, especially in light of the superior firepower and numbers they faced. Most portrayals of this nature include a trumpeter calling for Benteen. (Little Big Horn Battlefield National Monument)

the ridge. With barely more than 100 soldiers left, E and F companies were surrounded near Cemetery Ridge and Custer Hill. They were now outnumbered by as many as 15 or 20 to one and there was no sign of Reno or Benteen.

Both companies made their way toward the top of the hill. It was a poor position, with thousands of warriors moving in for the final attack. Exposed troopers were picked off, while groups of mounted warriors stampeded many of the Army horses. The Sioux managed to concentrate on the weakest points. They continued to attack by fire, to pin and suppress. Other warriors remained mounted and mobile.

The surviving members of Custer's command hunkered down behind dead horses as Indians further encroached on their position. Ammunition shortages could not have been a critical concern, for most Indian accounts testify that captured cartridge belts had ample rounds still on them. Custer may have been shot at this point, for a mounted foray was attempted without him. With the greater threat coming from the direction of Calhoun Hill to the south, E Company mounted what horses were still available, and made a dash toward the west. The E Company commander was left behind, dead or wounded on the hill. Whether to escape or to drive off enfilading snipers, the manoeuvre failed. Thousands of warriors diverted their movement into the Deep ravine.

About 50 men (F Company and right wing survivors) remained on Custer Hill. The numbers dwindled as Indian firepower took its toll. Finally a group of 15-20 dismounted soldiers desperately attempted to flee toward

This Cheyenne brave has seized the guidon of Calhoun's L Company. It may have been this event that Weir witnessed. Buffalo Calf Road Woman, who rides alongside him, rescued her brother Chief Comes-In-Sight at the Rosebud, and is reputed to have fought on horseback at the 'Greasy Grass'. Although most of the Crow Scouts had escaped before the battle-proper started, this Scout's appearance is fairly typical. (Illustration by Richard Hook)

View from Custer Hill looking south-west. The markers indicate where Lt.Col. George Armstrong Custer and 41 members of his regiment were found along with 39 dead horses. All the markers are on the western slope of the hill, 10-20 yards from the crest. The marker with a black crest on it indicates where Custer's body was first buried. The view from this spot includes the Little Big Horn Valley, where the immense Indian camp skirted the Little Big Horn River. (C. Thebaud)

E Company in the Deep Ravine. They were shot or ridden down, and their bodies lay scattered from the hill to the upper portions of the ravine.

THE END FOR CUSTER

'Soldiers were piled one on top of another, dead, and here and there an Indian among the soldiers.' RUNS THE ENEMY

The final event was an anti-climax to the battle. Those soldiers on Custer Hill who were wounded or did not attempt to flee were overrun by the victorious Sioux and Cheyenne. It is doubtful that any of Custer's group were left standing as warriors closed in to finish them off. There was some resistance, as a few warriors were killed in the final hand-to-hand melee.

Most portrayals of the final moments show too many soldiers on the hill, and include a trumpeter calling for Benteen. This is doubtful, because Wier, who could hear the shooting, would also have heard the bugle.

Custer was either dead or dying by this time. He was found on top of a soldier, and horse, shot in the chest, and then in the left temple. On the ground next to him were 17 shells from his Remmington sporting rifle. Nearby lay his brother Tom, shot full of arrows and his adjutant Lt. Cooke. Wooden Leg came and scalped Cooke's sideburns. Other dead lying around Custer included Trumpeter Voss, Boston Custer and Sgt. Hughes Farther, Custer's personal guidon bearer.

Capt. Yates and 2nd Lt. Reily, the Company F executive officer, were on the hill with about 20 other F Company troopers. Lt. Algernon Smith, E Company commander, was the only man from his company found on Custer Hill. There were 42 bodies on the hill and 39 dead horses. The 210 men of the Custer battalion were all killed. By 6.00 pm the mounted warriors were beginning to attack Wier and Benteen. Custer's troopers were stripped and mutilated by the warriors and women who stayed behind.

THE AFTERMATH

Capt. Thomas H. French was M Company commander under Reno. He survived the rout from the valley, and was instrumental in rallying the defeated battalion and establishing the hilltop defence. He survived to fight against the Nez Percé in 1877. (Brigham Young University Camp Collection)

The officers on Wier Point had unknowingly witnessed Custer's final moments, but as Lt. Godfrey described it, 'While watching this group, the conclusion was arrived at that Custer had been repulsed, and the firing was the parting shots of the rear guard. The firing ceased, the groups dispersed, clouds of dust rose from all parts of the field, and the horsemen converged toward our position.'

After a poorly executed withdrawal from Wier Point, with one wounded man abandoned, the surviving members of the 7th Cavalry re-established themselves on Reno Hill. Civilian scout Herendeen and 12 troopers, left stranded in the valley earlier, made their way to the hilltop that afternoon. Lt. DeRudio, Fred Girard and two others left in the valley also rejoined the command two days later. The surrounded soldiers dug-in on the hilltop with improvised tools, warding off all attacks from their shallow rifle pits. The packs were unloaded and used as makeshift breastworks. The Indians continued to snipe at them from a distance. Over 400 horses and mules were picketed on the exposed eastern edge of the position. Dozens of animals were shot where they stood.

All of the wounded were brought to a field hospital in a circular depression in the centre of the position. Shielded on three sides by high ground and the picket line of horses on the east, Dr. Porter (the only surviving surgeon) began to tend to the accumulating wounded. By nightfall on 25 June, there were five more killed and six more wounded. During the night a few warriors kept watch on the soldiers, but most were in the camp, which moved about a mile north, celebrating the victory. There was a brief rain shower that night. Those Indian families that had not re-erected their tepees since their afternoon scramble pitched temporary wickiups in preparation for a movement the next day.

On the morning of 26 June the Indians attacked again, but made no overwhelming aggressive attacks like those of the first day. They continued to snipe and infiltrate, causing 48 more casualties, including seven dead. Reno had 60 wounded by the end of the siege.

Benteen led H Company on a dismounted charge to the south. This limited counter-attack succeeded in driving off a menacing group of warriors who had encroached on the perimeter. Later a party of volunteers, covered by sharpshooter fire, made its way down 'Water Carriers' Ravine'

Victory Dance *by F.B. Fiske. The exultant Sioux and Cheyenne re-established their camp adjacent to its original sight, and celebrated their victory on the night of 25 June, while the 7th Cavalry survivors lay besieged on Reno Hill. After limited attacks on 26 June, the various hostile factions scattered.(Little Big Horn National Monument)*

to fill canteens for the thirsty soldiers. Several were awarded the Congressional Medal of Honour for this deed. With the surviving cavalry in protected positions and with ample ammunition the Indians were unable, or unwilling, to finish them off.

In the afternoon the Indians set fire to the prairie grass and broke camp. The soldiers on the hilltop watched. As Sergeant Charles Windolph described it, 'The heavy smoke seemed to lift for a few moments, and there in the valley below we caught glimpses of thousands of Indians on foot and horseback, with their pony herds and travois, dogs and pack animals, and all the trappings of a great camp, slowly moving southward. It was like some Biblical Exodus; the Israelites moving into Egypt; a mighty tribe on the march.' Reno buried his dead and repositioned closer to the river that evening.

Word of Terry's approaching column had reached the camp on the 26 June, but by the time Gen. Terry's column arrived, on 27 June, the Indian tribes had scattered and the large camp was gone. It was the Indians' greatest victory over the whites, and the last.

TERRY'S ARRIVAL

General Terry, with Gibbon's Montana Column, had been over a day's march north during the battle, and still several miles away before nightfall on 26 June. By this time Gibbon had recovered from his intestinal virus and was back in the saddle. They did not approach the battlefield until 27 June, and then with great caution.

The hostiles were fully aware of his advance, and were prepared to give battle. (They also had about 200 additional Springfield carbines and captured ammunition.) At one point Terry's troopers thought they had met Custer's regiment. However, the blue-coated column, flying a

Beecher's Island *by Robert Lindneux. This gives some idea of the conditions on Reno Hill during the siege. Reno's command, joined by Benteen and the pack train dug in on Reno Hill and were fired on continuously until late on 26 June. (Robert Lindneux)*

stars-and-stripes guidon, was Sioux, wearing trophies from the Battle of the Greasy Grass. They tried to induce combat with Terry's column but without success. Terry had received some indication of the defeat from a few of Custer's fleeing scouts, but had disregarded the report.

When the lead elements of the 2nd Cavalry arrived at the abandoned Indian campsites it was an incredible and grotesque scene. The entire area was burned out, and smoke and the smell of decaying flesh hung in the air. Dead or suffering animals littered the area along with countless piles of food, debris and discarded possessions. When they began to find the horses, clothing, personal effects, severed heads and bodies of 7th Cavalry troopers, there was grave concern.

There were many lodge poles and wickiups, but only three covered tepees were standing. These were burial sites. An excess of abandoned items led to the false assumption that the Montana column chased away the hostiles, and rescued the 7th Cavalry.

Lt. Bradley, Gibbon's chief of scouts, was the first to report the bloated corpses from Custer's battalion. His message to Terry read: 'Up to this time I have counted 200 dead officers and soldiers. I have never met Custer, but from photographs which I have seen of him I think one of the bodies is the General's.' Terry could make out the bodies from his position in the valley.

Terry was met by Hare and Wallace, who asked, 'What has become of Custer's five troops? They left us yesterday and we have not seen or heard anything of them since. The last we saw of him he was going down the high bluff toward the lower end of the village.'

Terry, still in shock from the news, told them, 'From information I have received, I have good reason to believe they are all dead up there on the ridge.' For the next two days Terry ordered burial of the dead and destruction of Indian property, and made preparations for moving the 60 wounded men. Mule litters were constructed for the wounded, and the column took two days to march 12 miles to the mouth of the Little Big Horn. The ponderous column was extremely vulnerable, but there was very little Indian activity. Captain Grant Marsh had navigated the steamer *Far West* up the

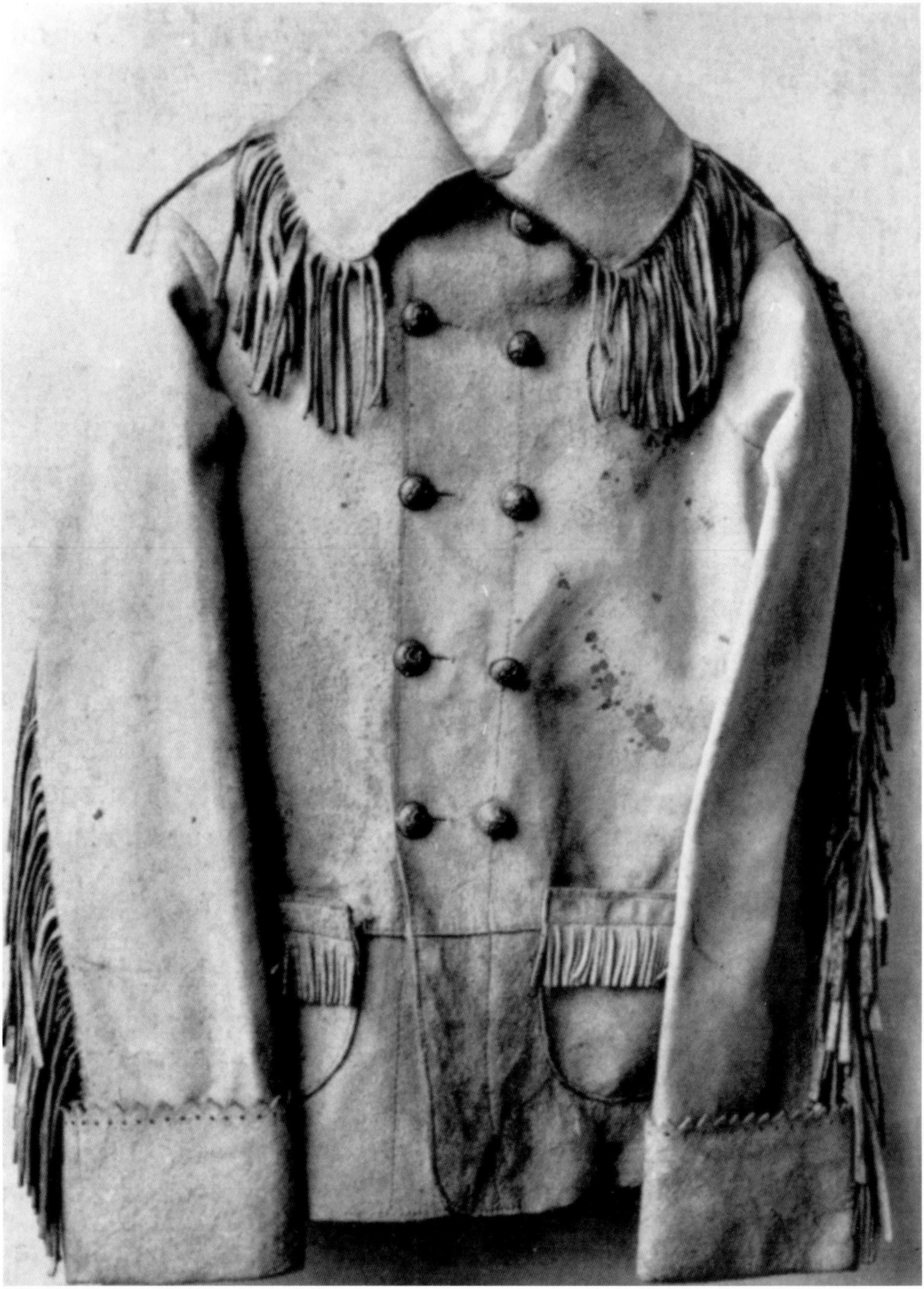

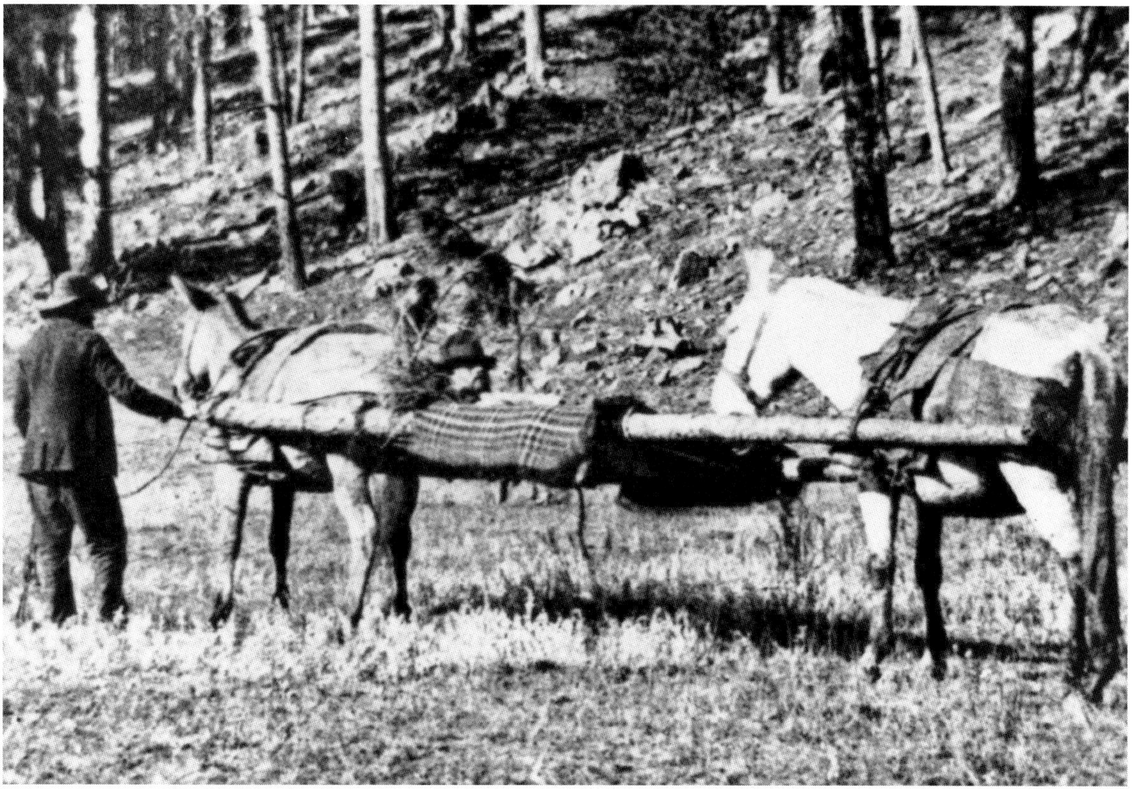

The wounded from Reno's Command traversed difficult terrain to arrive at Far West, *which was waiting at the fork of the Big Horn and Little Big Horn Rivers. (Library of Congress)*

Big Horn, and on 30 June the wounded and the Gatling guns were uploaded. The remnants of the 7th Cavalry combined with the 2nd under Gibbon, and all departed for the Fort Pease supply base. Thus the Montana column had 'rescued' the 7th Cavalry.

A FAILED CAMPAIGN

When the *Far West* was prepared on 3 July to carry the wounded to Fort Lincoln, General Terry confided his feelings of guilt to the boat's captain. 'Every soldier here who is suffering with wounds is a victim of a terrible blunder, a sad and terrible blunder.' The steamer reached Bismark, Dakota Territory, 710 miles down the Yellowstone and Missouri Rivers in an unsurpassed record of 54 hours. A shocked American public, celebrating the centennial, received news of 'the Custer Massacre'. Politicians, newspapers, and the public called for an explanation from the Army, and immediate action to subdue and punish the hostiles.

As for investigating the 'blunder', Generals Terry and Sheridan both submitted reports in grand revisionist fashion – 'tragic examples of official misconceived history'. Both subtly allowed Custer, Reno and Benteen to wrestle for tactical blame, ignoring the complete operational failure they had fostered.

There was to be little satisfaction for the Indians, who evaded the Army that summer, but eventually suffered extensively from future maltreatment

LEFT *Custer's buckskin jacket. Custer was famous for his flamboyant dress throughout the American Civil War, and he carried on the practice of self-styled uniforms until his death. (Little Big Horn Battlefield National Monument)*

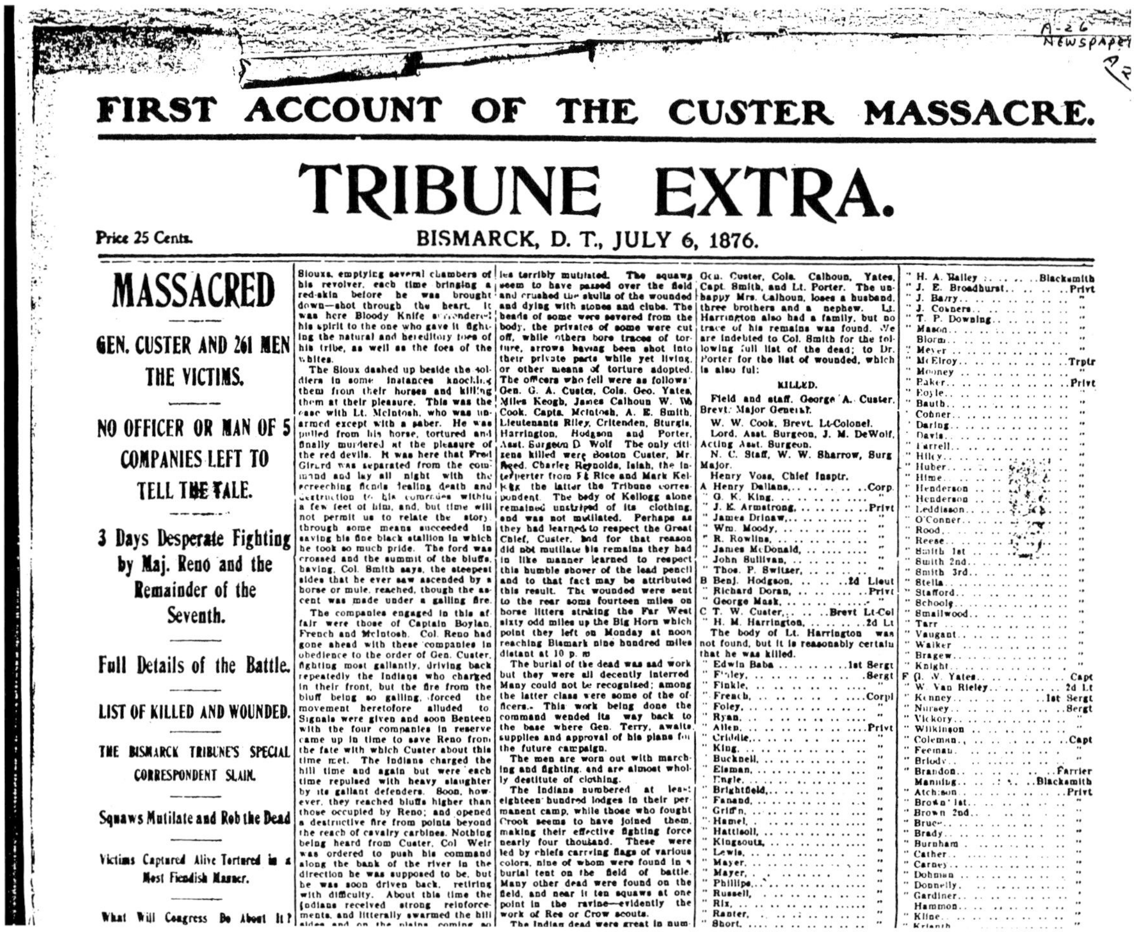

FIRST ACCOUNT OF THE CUSTER MASSACRE.

TRIBUNE EXTRA.

Price 25 Cents. BISMARCK, D. T., JULY 6, 1876.

MASSACRED

GEN. CUSTER AND 261 MEN THE VICTIMS.

NO OFFICER OR MAN OF 5 COMPANIES LEFT TO TELL THE TALE.

3 Days Desperate Fighting by Maj. Reno and the Remainder of the Seventh.

Full Details of the Battle.

LIST OF KILLED AND WOUNDED.

THE BISMARCK TRIBUNE'S SPECIAL CORRESPONDENT SLAIN.

Squaws Mutilate and Rob the Dead

Victims Captured Alive Tortured in a Most Fiendish Manner.

What Will Congress Do About It?

Siouxs, emptying several chambers of his revolver, each time bringing a red-skin before he was brought down—shot through the heart. It was here Bloody Knife surrendered his spirit to the one who gave it fighting the natural and hereditary foes of his tribe, as well as the foes of the whites.

The Sioux dashed up beside the soldiers in some instances knocking them from their horses and killing them at their pleasure. This was the case with Lt. McIntosh, who was unarmed except with a saber. He was pulled from his horse, tortured and finally murdered at the pleasure of the red devils. It was here that Fred Girard was separated from the command and lay all night with the screeching fiends dealing death and destruction to his comrades within a few feet of him, and, but time will not permit us to relate the story, through some means succeeded in saving his fine black stallion in which he took so much pride. The ford was crossed and the summit of the bluffs, having, Col. Smith says, the steepest sides that he ever saw ascended by a horse or mule, reached, though the ascent was made under a galling fire.

The companies engaged in this affair were those of Captain Boylan, French and McIntosh. Col. Reno had gone ahead with these companies in obedience to the order of Gen. Custer, fighting most gallantly, driving back repeatedly the Indians who charged in their front, but the fire from the bluff being so galling, forced the movement heretofore alluded to. Signals were given and soon Benteen with the four companies in reserve came up in time to save Reno from the fate with which Custer about this time met. The Indians charged the hill time and again but were each time repulsed with heavy slaughter by its gallant defenders. Soon, however, they reached bluffs higher than those occupied by Reno; and opened a destructive fire from points beyond the reach of cavalry carbines. Nothing being heard from Custer, Col Weir was ordered to push his command along the bank of the river in the direction he was supposed to be, but he was soon driven back, retiring with difficulty. About this time the Indians received strong reinforcements, and litterally swarmed the hill [illegible]

ies terribly mutilated. The squaws seem to have passed over the field and crushed the skulls of the wounded and dying with stones and clubs. The heads of some were severed from the body, the privates of some were cut off, while others bore traces of torture, arrows having been shot into their private parts while yet living, or other means of torture adopted. The officers who fell were as follows: Gen. G. A. Custer, Cols. Geo. Yates, Miles Keogh, James Calhoun W. W. Cook. Capts. McIntosh, A. E. Smith, Lieutenants Riley, Critenden, Sturgis, Harrington, Hodgson and Porter, Asst. Surgeon D. Wolf. The only citizens killed were Boston Custer, Mr. Reed, Charles Reynolds, Isiah, the interperter from Ft Rice and Mark Kellogg the latter the Tribune correspondent. The body of Kellogg alone remained unstriped of its clothing, and was not mutilated. Perhaps as they had learned to respect the Great Chief, Custer, and for that reason did not mutilate his remains they had in like manner learned to respect this humble shover of the lead pencil and to that fact may be attributed this result. The wounded were sent to the rear some fourteen miles on horse litters striking the Far West sixty odd miles up the Big Horn which point they left on Monday at noon reaching Bismark nine hundred miles distant at 10 p. m.

The burial of the dead was sad work but they were all decently interred. Many could not be recognised; among the latter class were some of the officers. This work being done the command wended its way back to the base where Gen. Terry, awaits supplies and approval of his plans for the future campaign.

The men are worn out with marching and fighting, and are almost wholly destitute of clothing.

The Indians numbered at least eighteen hundred lodges in their permanent camp, while those who fought Crook seems to have joined them, making their effective fighting force nearly four thousand. These were led by chiefs carrying flags of various colors, nine of whom were found in a burial tent on the field of battle. Many other dead were found on the field, and near it ten squaws at one point in the ravine—evidently the work of Ree or Crow scouts.

Gen. Custer, Cols. Calhoun, Yates, Capt. Smith, and Lt. Porter. The unhappy Mrs. Calhoun, loses a husband, three brothers and a nephew. Lt. Harrington also had a family, but no trace of his remains was found. We are indebted to Col. Smith for the following full list of the dead; to Dr. Porter for the list of wounded, which is also ful:

KILLED.

Field and staff. George A. Custer, Brevt. Major General.

W. W. Cook, Brevt. Lt-Colonel.

Lord, Asst. Surgeon, J. M. DeWolf, Acting Asst. Surgeon.

N. C. Staff, W. W. Sharrow, Surg Major.

Henry Voss, Chief Insptr.

A Henry Dallans, ... Corp.
" G. K. King, ... "
" J. K. Armstrong, ... Privt
" James Drinaw, ... "
" Wm. Moody, ... "
" R. Rowlins, ... "
" James McDonald, ... "
" John Sullivan, ... "
" Thos. P. Switser, ... "
B Benj. Hodgson, ... 2d Lieut
" Richard Doran, ... Privt
" George Mask, ... "
C T. W. Custer, ... Brevt Lt-Col
" H. M. Harrington, ... 2d Lt

The body of Lt. Harrington was not found, but it is reasonably certain that he was killed.

" Edwin Baba .. .. 1st Sergt
" Finley, ... Sergt
" Finkle, ... "
" French, ... Corpl
" Foley, ... "
" Ryan, ... "
" Allen, ... Privt
" Criddle, ... "
" King, ... "
" Bucknell, ... "
" Eisman, ... "
" Engle, ... "
" Brightfield, ... "
" Fanand, ... "
" Griffin, ... "
" Hamel, ... "
" Hattisoll, ... "
" Kingsouts, ... "
" Lewis, ... "
" Mayer, ... "
" Mayer, ... "
" Phillips, ... "
" Russell, ... "
" Rix, ... "
" Ranter, ... "
" Short, ... "

" H. A. Bailey .. .. Blacksmith
" J. E. Broadhurst .. .. Privt
" J. Barry .. .. "
" J. Conners .. .. "
" T. P. Downing .. .. "
" Mason .. .. "
Blorm .. .. "
" Meyer .. .. "
" McElroy .. .. Trptr
" Mooney .. .. "
" Baker .. .. Privt
" Boyle .. .. "
" Bauth .. .. "
" Cobner .. .. "
" Darling .. .. "
" Davis .. .. "
" Farrell .. .. "
" Hiley .. .. "
" Huber .. .. "
" Hime .. .. "
" Henderson .. .. "
" Henderson .. .. "
" Leddisson .. .. "
" O'Conner .. .. "
" Rood .. .. "
" Reese .. .. "
" Smith 1st .. .. "
" Smith 2nd .. .. "
" Smith 3rd .. .. "
" Stella .. .. "
" Stafford .. .. "
" Schoole .. .. "
" Smallwood .. .. "
" Tarr .. .. "
" Vaugant .. .. "
" Walker .. .. "
" Bragew .. .. "
" Knight .. .. "
F G. W. Yates .. .. Capt
" W. Van Rieley .. .. 2d Lt
" Kenney .. .. 1st Sergt
" Nursey .. .. Sergt
" Vickory .. .. "
" Wilkinson .. .. "
" Coleman .. .. Capt
" Feeman .. .. "
" Briody .. .. "
" Brandon .. .. Farrier
Manning .. .. Blacksmith
" Atchison .. .. Privt
" Brown 1st .. .. "
" Brown 2nd .. .. "
" Bruce .. .. "
" Brady .. .. "
" Burnham .. .. "
" Cather .. .. "
" Carney .. .. "
" Dohman .. .. "
" Donnelly .. .. "
" Gardiner .. .. "
Hammon .. .. "
" Kline .. .. "

By 6 July 1876, the entire world had learned of the 'Custer massacre'. The Media, no different to today, thrived on such sensational stories and printed both fact and fiction to a believing public. One of the more interesting headlines is 'What will Congress do about it?' (U.S. National Archives)

at the hands of the US Government. Neither Crook nor Terry would venture from their supply bases for over a month. Sheridan admonished Crook to 'hit them again and hit them hard!', but both field commanders waited for more troops to commence operations. Both restarted their expeditions the first week in August with ample reinforcements; Terry had 1700 infantry and cavalry and Crook 2300.

During this time the various massed camps celebrated their victory near the Big Horn Mountains. Some Indians expected to be left alone as a result of their victory (as after Red Cloud's War), while others feared a white backlash and returned to the reservations. Gradually the larger camps migrated back toward the Rosebud region. The larger followings split into their tribal factions in early August near the mouth of the Powder River. Many of the Cheyenne returned south along the Powder River toward Wyoming. The Sans Arc Sioux went north-west, crossing the Yellowstone River, and Sitting Bull continued north-east toward the Little Missouri River.

Both Army columns followed stale trails and converged, by accident, along the Rosebud on 10 August. The 4000-man combined army remained together, under Terry's command, and followed the month-old Indian trail.

SUMMER PURSUIT, JULY-SEPTEMBER 1876

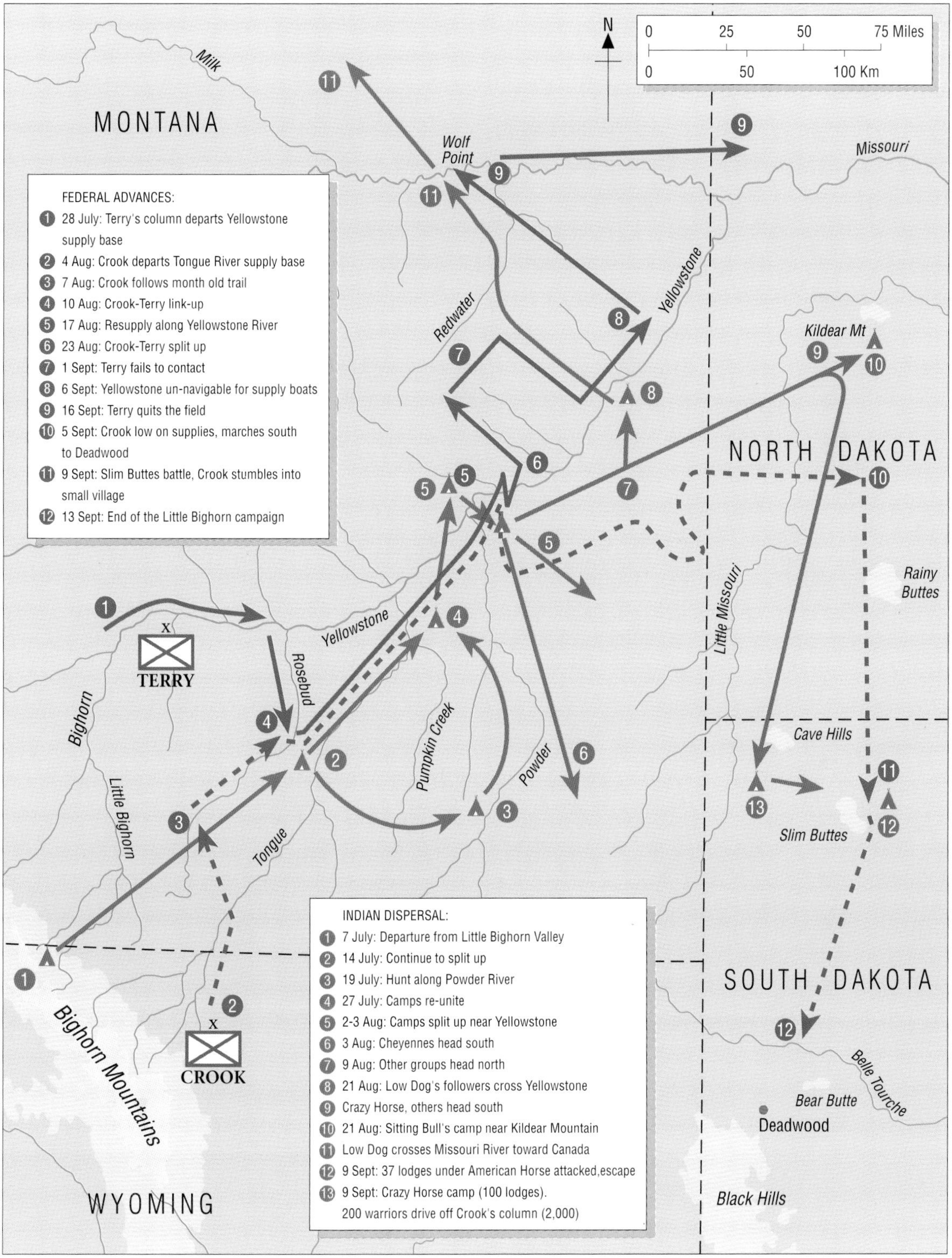

N
0 25 50 75 Miles
0 50 100 Km
MONTANA
Milk
Wolf Point
Missouri
Yellowstone
Redwater
Kildear Mt
NORTH DAKOTA
Rainy Buttes
Little Missouri
Cave Hills
Slim Buttes
SOUTH DAKOTA
Belle Fourche
Bear Butte
Deadwood
Black Hills
TERRY
CROOK
Bighorn
Little Bighorn
Rosebud
Tongue
Pumpkin Creek
Powder
Bighorn Mountains
WYOMING
FEDERAL ADVANCES:
1 28 July: Terry's column departs Yellowstone supply base
2 4 Aug: Crook departs Tongue River supply base
3 7 Aug: Crook follows month old trail
4 10 Aug: Crook-Terry link-up
5 17 Aug: Resupply along Yellowstone River
6 23 Aug: Crook-Terry split up
7 1 Sept: Terry fails to contact
8 6 Sept: Yellowstone un-navigable for supply boats
9 16 Sept: Terry quits the field
10 5 Sept: Crook low on supplies, marches south to Deadwood
11 9 Sept: Slim Buttes battle, Crook stumbles into small village
12 13 Sept: End of the Little Bighorn campaign
INDIAN DISPERSAL:
1 7 July: Departure from Little Bighorn Valley
2 14 July: Continue to split up
3 19 July: Hunt along Powder River
4 27 July: Camps re-unite
5 2-3 Aug: Camps split up near Yellowstone
6 3 Aug: Cheyennes head south
7 9 Aug: Other groups head north
8 21 Aug: Low Dog's followers cross Yellowstone
9 Crazy Horse, others head south
10 21 Aug: Sitting Bull's camp near Kildear Mountain
11 Low Dog crosses Missouri River toward Canada
12 9 Sept: 37 lodges under American Horse attacked,escape
13 9 Sept: Crazy Horse camp (100 lodges). 200 warriors drive off Crook's column (2,000)

Native American artwork rendition of the 1877 stabbing of Crazy Horse while he was being taken into confinement. Crazy Horse was a symbol of fanatical defiance and uncompromising resistance, even after his death. (Amos Bad Heart Buffalo)

By mid-August Crazy Horse and most of the Oglala Sioux split from Sitting Bull's camp and cut south to the Black Hills. Crazy Horse raided the miners in the Black Hills while far to the west a massive Army force found nothing. The combined columns rapidly depleted their supplies and had to wait near the Yellowstone for replenishment. Relations between the two commanders were 'less than co-operative'.

Crook had his column depart the joint bivouac without notice on 22 August. With limited supplies he set out to follow Sitting Bull's trail. Terry followed another trail but cancelled operations due to logistical shortages and the fact that the rivers were becoming un-navigable. By 3 September Crook had found nothing. He had again depleted his food and forage, beginning what was referred to as his 'starvation march'. He abandoned the trail and forced-marched south to get emergency supplies at Deadwood in the Black Hills. Crook's advanced party stumbled onto the camp of the Oglala Sioux American Horse, near Slim Buttes (which is on the Sioux Reservation). The troopers attacked, with minimal results. Crazy Horse counter-attacked from his camp nearby, pinning Crook's entire force with less than 300 warriors. Crook was disinterested in pursuit, and continued south to Deadwood, ending the campaign.

The US Congress authorised Sheridan to impose military rule on the reservations, disarming, dismounting and subjugating all of the Agency Indians. The roamers would no longer be able to count on Agency Indian support. The Black Hills, the 'unceded territory', and much of the Sioux Reservation was also appropriated through sale or outright forfeiture.

The Army launched several extensively resourced winter campaigns, and increased their use of armed Indian allies and scouts. Winter expeditions under Colonels Nelson A. Miles and R. S. Mackenzie attacked and relentlessly pursued the Sioux and Cheyenne roamers. By the spring of 1877 the roamers were forced to return to the reservation in great numbers. On 6 May 1877 Crazy Horse surrendered with 1100 followers. Crazy

Spotted Eagle, majestic chief of the Sans-Arc Sioux, was a prominent leader and a fierce warrior. He and his followers fled into Canada with Sitting Bull. In 1880, with the buffalo herds depleted, he and his people went south and surrendered to General Nelson A. Miles. (Little Big Horn Battlefield National Monument)

Horse proved to be too unruly for 'confined conditions'. A few months later, while he was under arrest, he was bayoneted and killed. The last operations of the Great Sioux War were over.

SITTING BULL'S DEFIANCE

Sitting Bull's remaining 400 Hunkpapas and the Sans Arc Sioux led by Spotted Eagle fled north across the border into Canada. As Rain in the Face put it, 'We moved camp north. They followed many days till we crossed the line [into Canada]. I stayed over there till Sitting Bull came back and I came back with him.' With the buffalo diminishing, and the Army patrolling the border, the exiled warriors were eventually starved or deprived into submission. Gall, Crow King and numerous other leaders came in with their bands. In 1880 Spotted Eagle followed suit, and in July 1881 Sitting Bull and a tiny remnant of his once massive following came to Fort Buford on the Missouri River. He said to the post commander, 'I wish it to be remembered that I was the last man of my tribe to surrender my rifle, this day have I given it to you.'

THE BATTLEFIELD TODAY

The Little Big Horn Battlefield National Monument, formerly called the Custer Battlefield, lies within the Crow reservation in south-eastern Montana. Interstate Highway 90 (I-90) crosses the Little Big Horn one mile to the west of the park. US Highway 212 connects the monument with the Black Hills and Yellowstone National Parks. The Crow Agency is two miles north, and the town of Hardin, Montana, is 18 miles north. The nearest commercial airport is at Billings, Montana, 65 miles north-west on I-95.

Despite its remote location, the Little Big Horn battlefield is an extremely popular tourist spot and has an excellent visitor centre and bookshop. Maintained by the US Department of the Interior National Park Service, it is superbly set up for preservation, observation, and homage to the Native Americans, the 7th Cavalry, and the additional 5,000 veterans and dependants buried in the national cemetery that was established there in 1879. The National Park grounds are limited to the Custer Battlefield and the much smaller Reno-Benteen Battlefield 4.5 miles south. There is a fee to enter the park.

The city most advantageous for local study of the Sioux Wars, and other battlefields is Sheridan, Wyoming. Located 70 miles south of the Little Big Horn battlefield, Sheridan is the site of Crook's northern supply base. From Sheridan one can easily visit the Rosebud battlefield, Fort Phil Kearny, and the locations of the Wagon Box and Fetterman battles.

CHRONOLOGY

Crow King, Hunkpapa Sioux, was reported, along with Gall and Crazy Horse, to have been one of the 'ruling spirits' in directing the other bands to defeat the divided 7th Cavalry. He had a large personal following – about 80 warriors. (Little Big Horn Battlefield National Monument)

Events leading up to the Battle of the Little Big Horn
(Indian activity in italics)

1875

9 November 1875 – Inspector E.C. Watkins' report.
6 December – Ultimatum issued: 'Report to Agency or be considered hostile'.
15 December – *Start of famine on Great Sioux Reservation.*

1876

18 January 1876 – Embargo on sale of arms and ammunition on reservations.
31 January – Deadline for return to reservations.
8 Febuary – Sheridan orders Terry and Crook to 'prepare for operations against the hostiles'.
1 March – Crook departs Fort Fetterman.
16 March – Crook/Reynolds move up Powder River.
17 March – Reynolds attacks Indian Village on Little Powder River, Montana.
24 March – *Powder River survivors combine with Crazy Horse camp.*
26 March – Crook's column returns to Fort Fetterman.
1 April – Col. Gibbon's Montana Column departs Fort Ellis.
8 April – *Winter roamers combine with Sitting Bull camp near Chalk Butte.*
20 April – *Sans Arcs join camp at head of Sheep Creek.*
22 April – *First sign of new grass for Indian ponies.*
26 April – *Santees and Cheyenne arrive at camp on Powder River at Mizpah.*
28 April – *Abundant new grass for ponies.*
3 May – *First of raids on Gibbon, Crow scout's ponies stolen.*
5 May – *Kill Eagle arrives at Tongue River camp at mouth of Pumpkin Creek.*
11 May – *Cheyenne arrive at Tongue River camp at Ash Creek.*
15 May Lt. Bradley locates main Sioux camp, 35 miles from Gibbon.
17 May – Gibbon fails to cross Yellowstone, cancels attack on main camp. Terry's Dakota Column departs Fort Abraham Lincoln.
19 May – *Indians camp close to Yellowstone hunting buffalo. Gibbon hears firing.*
22 May – *Cheyenne arrive at camp on Rosebud Creek.*
23 May – Lt. Bradley locates main camp 18 miles from Gibbon.

24 May – *Attacks on Gibbon continue.*

27 May – Gibbon sends sketchy report to Terry.

29 May – Crook's column departs Fort Fetterman.

31 May – Terry's column crosses the Little Missouri River.

1 June – Snowstorm strikes the region.

5 June – *Sun Dance at camp on Rosebud River.*

8 June – Terry finds Gibbon along the Yellowstone.

9 June – *Raid on Crook's Tongue River depot from camp on Muddy Creek.*

10 June – Maj. Reno's scout from Powder River depot.

16 June – *Warriors depart to attack Crook from camp on Reno Creek.*

17 June – *The Battle of The Rosebud, Montana; Crook attacked by Crazy Horse.*

18 June – Crook withdraws from campaign to await reinforcements.

19 June – *Warriors celebrating Rosebud battle at camp on Little Big Horn.*

19 June – Reno returns from scout of Powder and Rosebud rivers.

23 June – *Influx of summer roamers at Little Big Horn Camp.*

21 June – Terry holds strategy conference aboard the steamer Far West.

22 June – Terry releases Custer and 7th Cavalry Regiment to move independently.

23 June – Custer is 47 miles up Rosebud. Terry has not crossed south of Yellowstone River.

24 June – Custer at mouth of Davis Creek. Terry halts at mouth of Tullock Creek. Custer orders a night march toward the Little Big Horn.

24 June – *Cheyenne arrive at new camp on Little Big Horn.*

25 JUNE BATTLE OF THE LITTLE BIG HORN

0300 – Custer halts 7th Cav., Davis Creek

0845 – Resumes advance

1212 – Custer divides 7th Cav. to advance as three battalions.

1410 – Cavalry sees fleeing Cheyenne band from Lone Tepee

1415 – Custer gives Reno order to pursue

1430 – Benteen rejoins Custer trail in Reno Creek

1440 – Benteen waters horses at the morass

1455 – Custer turns north onto high ground seperating from Reno. Reno fords Little Big Horn River.

1503 – Benteen departs the morass as pack train arrives

1505 – Reno advances and then charges

1515 – Reno halts, dismounts and forms skirmish line. Custer at Weir Point sees Reno

Native American artwork of mounted braves before the battle. This event as depicted is highly symbolic, but it does indicate the dress and armament of the Indians. Although there are no accounts of Crazy Horse's 'trooping of the line', he did delay his engagement with Custer's battalion for 10-15 minutes while performing a pre-battle spiritual ritual. (Amos Bad Heart Buffalo)

Trumpeter Giovanni Martini, an Italian immigrant who had anglicised his name to John Martin. He carried Custer's last message to Benteen, but was unable to elaborate or effectively communicate the situation. Martin was the last trooper to see the Custer battalion alive. (Little Big Horn Battlefield National Monument)

1520 – Custer sends Martin to fetch Benteen
1530 – Reno withdraws to treeline
1545 – Custer reaches top of Medicine Tail Coulee
1555 – Reno retreats towards river
1605 – First of fleeing troopers reach Reno Hill
1610 – Stragglers reach Reno Hill Custer's Left Wing recons ford.
1620 – Benteen reaches Reno Hill. Custer's Left Wing disengages from ford.
1630 – Custer's Bn. links up at Calhoun Hill
1650 – Weir departs Reno Hill with D Co.
1712 – Benteen departs Reno Hill with H, K, M Cos.
1715 – Custer's Right Wing collapses. Pack Train reaches Reno Hill
1720 – D Co. reaches Weir Point
1730 – Custer's position collapses
1750 – Reno follows Benteen with A, B, G Cos.
1800 – Retreat from Weir Point begins
1830 – Reassemble on Reno Hill

26 June – *Warriors continue to besiege Reno Hill. Camp moves upstream in evening.*
27 June – Gen. Terry's column arrives, Indians have departed.
7 July – Skirmish at head of Tongue River.
9 September – Battle of Slim Buttes, Dakota. Crook attacks Indian village. Driven off by 200 warriors. Crook continues south to Deadwood, effectively ending campaign

(Compiled from various sources, primarily Gray, John S).

GUIDE TO FURTHER READING

The following list reviews those recommended works that are readily available and were of greatest influence on this publication.

Fox, Richard A., *Archaeology, History, and Custer's Last Battle,* Univ. of Oklahoma Press, 1993. Without question the definitive account of the most debated part of the fight.

Gray, John S., *Centennial Campaign, the Sioux War of 1876,* Univ. of Oklahoma Press, 1988. The best work available for factual clarification of the entire campaign.

Darling, Roger, *A Sad and Terrible Blunder, Generals Terry and Custer on the Little Big Horn: New Discoveries,* Potomac Western Press, 1990. Priceless in 'correcting a century of misconceived history'.

Utley, Robert M. *Cavalier in Buckskin,* Univ. of Oklahoma Press, 1988. Utley is considered the top Custer biographer, and this work is highly recommended.

Sarf, Wayne M. *The Little Big Horn Campaign, March-September 1876,* Combined Books, 1993. An excellent reference.

Urwin, Gregory, *Custer Victorious: The Civil War Battles of General George Armstrong Custer,* University of Nebraska Press, 1983. A real understanding and appreciation of Custer.

Hammer, Kenneth M. (Ed.) *Custer in '76: Walter Camp's Notes on the Custer Fight,* BYU Press, 1976. A useful source, and invaluable interviews by Walter Camp.

Katcher, Philip, *The American Indian Wars 1860-1890,* Men-at-Arms 63, Osprey, 1977.

Hook, Jason, *The American Plains Indians, Men-at-Arms 163,* Osprey, 1985.

Katcher, Philip, *US Cavalry on the Plains 1850-1890,* Men-at-Arms 168, Osprey, 1985.

Pegler, Martin, *US Cavalryman 1865-1890, Warrior 4,* Osprey, 1993.

The Little Big Horn Associates (P.O. Box 640286, El Paso, TX 79904) Describing itself as 'an organisation dedicated to seeking the truth about the famous battle and all aspects of the settlement of the West'. Membership includes receipt of the bi-annual Research Review and a newsletter ten months a year.

Little Big Man, Oglala Sioux, a staunch supporter of Crazy Horse and one of his most hot-blooded warriors. He was not a chief, but so respected and well recognised that in combat warriors flocked to follow him. He was considered irreconcilable, but by 1877 he was an agency policeman, involved in Crazy Horse's death. (Michael Her Many Horses)

INDEX

(References to illustrations are shown in **bold**.)